CATCHING UNICORNS

C000156097

Compiled by Clodagh O'Reilly

Edited by Clodagh O'Reilly & Megan Bowden

In collaboration with the Association for Business Psychology
(theabp.org.uk) Workforce Experience Awards

Contents

Introduction

Organisations are undergoing disruption in every sphere. Demographic changes, increased globalisation and advancing technology are exponentially amplifying consumer, market and industry pressures. For many large organisations, remaining competitive requires tremendous agility.

Most organisations are underperforming in this respect. A survey by Chartered Global Management Accountant (CGMA) found that ineffective human capital management resulted in 43% of employers failing to achieve key financial targets, 40% having a reduced ability to innovate and 37% being unable to start a major project or strategic initiative. Similarly, Deloitte research found seven-in-ten global organisations felt they lacked the required skills to compete. An Accenture report indicated two-thirds of CEOs anticipated losing business to competitors due to talent gaps.

Collectively this presents a significant challenge, the response to which I believe lies in Assessment. To address the scale of this challenge and opportunity however, one needs to go beyond references to Assessment that may strike a traditional and dated chord. One needs to embrace holistic workforce measurement as a key to workforce optimisation.

To make a start, however, I encourage all organisations to adopt robust approaches to assessment whenever and wherever they can. And I am an advocate of Business Psychology for this purpose. Business Psychology is the study and practice of improving working life. It combines an understanding of the science of human behaviour with experience of the world of work, to attain effective and sustainable performance for both individuals and organisations. When focused on Assessment, Business Psychology Practitioners can add value in organisations that really moves the needle in terms of return on investment and workforce success.

This book shares examples of how assessment has been used to support organisations' success. It shares the experiences of some of the United Kingdom's best Business Psychology Practitioners in case studies which demonstrate how Business Psychology works, in practice, to improve organisational performance.

There are many professionals who recognise the value of applying science in their work with people, and who are looking for practical ways to do this. I hope the case studies collected here will help them find their way. For experienced Practitioners, I hope they will apply this content to benchmarking their practice; perhaps also finding new ideas to try.

Each case study has been peer reviewed and evaluated based on its reflection of the practice of Business Psychology, effective application of conceptual business and psychological models and validated, evidenced impact.

As you review each case you will find an **overview** by way of introduction to the case study. You may use this to ascertain the case's relevance to your work, as it typically describes the context for the intervention. Next, the organisational **challenge,** presented to the Business Psychology Practitioners, is described. The **approach** taken by the Practitioners is then explained, with relevant references to knowledge, tools, and/or techniques used in response to the challenge. Finally, we share the **outcome** achieved for the organisation. This demonstrates the validity of the intervention by presenting evidence of positive commercial and/or behavioural impact.

As these case studies have been collected from many Practitioners, we also include acknowledgements of the organisations and Practitioners who shared their stories or directly contributed to the intervention's success. Case studies have been edited for presentation purposes, but as far as possible we retain and share the originator's tone and sentiment.

Contents

The case studies in this book are organised into four sections.

First, we consider standard assessment approaches, good examples of sound assessment practice in recruitment settings. These cases demonstrate how similar tools and models can be applied in different settings, to achieve diverse organisational priorities. They also vary in how they measure success, which can be informative for those looking to set standards for themselves.

Second, we consider those who have used typical approaches in more sophisticated ways. They may have combined multiple approaches, introduced innovations in their development or delivery model, or showed creativity in applying their findings. Perhaps their ideas will build confidence in the reader to stretch their thinking.

Third, we look at examples of employee assessment. Whilst the majority of structured and robust assessment tool use typically takes place during recruitment, those using similar approaches to collecting objective employee insight can get great value from doing so. Hopefully these cases will help advance the reader's thinking on the subject, if this is not something they're already doing.

Finally, we look to assessment interventions applied in broader and more ambitious settings. Here communities or large populations are being helped through assessment-based insights, and we learn interesting lessons. So perhaps these examples will serve to inspire thinking about the scale on which rigorous assessment practice can have an impact.

I conclude with some thoughts on the future of Assessment. I believe organisations today have both the imperatives and enablers to create inclusive meritocratic talent measurement solutions. But many organisations use validated assessments of worker ability on a very limited scale. So, I offer some provocation on 'what's next,' describing the emerging future of workforce insight I anticipate we could see.

If Assessment as a topic is entirely new to you, you may find it useful to reference the Appendix, "An Introduction to Assessment."

The case studies in this book refer to many Business Psychology theories, models and tools, applied to better understanding individuals. Not surprisingly a few are referenced multiple times, as they are well suited to many applications. Please note however that the inclusion of a reference to a model or a tool in this book is not an endorsement. The reader is encouraged to apply best practice and good judgement if electing to use any tools referenced here.

Acknowledgement

The case studies shared in this book have been collected by the Association for Business Psychology through the Workforce Experience Awards programme.

The Association was established in the United Kingdom twenty years ago, with the primary purpose of championing Business Psychology. It is a professional body which represents a community of Practitioners, researchers and academics who apply Business Psychology in the world of work. The membership includes Occupational, Industrial and Organisational Psychologists as well as professionals from other specialist disciplines such as Organisational Development, Talent Management, Coaching, Training, Human Resources and many more.

The Awards provide a credible platform for recording and recognising excellent practice in Business Psychology, allowing for the dissemination of leading Practitioners' knowledge and experience. It increases the visibility of the practice of Business Psychology to benefit organisations and Practitioners working in this field.

The Association has a well-established reputation for openness and support amongst members. Association events typically represent genuine knowledge-sharing in the interest of furthering the study and practice of Business Psychology.

This book is one in a series of three. It addresses Assessment interventions specifically, whilst the other publications address Business Psychology applied to improved Business Performance (Managed Metamorphosis) and Employee Experience (Stars Aligned).

With special thanks to Paul Carey for his input to this second edition.

Cover image by ERIN DIETSCHE

Section One:
Getting the Basics Right

In this section we share a selection of case studies which represent sound assessment practice in recruitment settings.

In the first case study, the selection of students for medical courses is addressed. Here the Business Psychologists enabled universities to consider applicants' non-academic attributes, such as integrity and empathy, which are essential to quality patient care.

In the second we hear from Fire and Rescue Services and their response to evolving demands placed on modern firefighters. This is an example of how collaborating across multiple organisations can bring shared benefits, economically.

Moving then to Banking, and a case study from The Royal Bank of Scotland. Find out how they addressed their need to hire top talent who would sustain the Bank's cultural values.

Fourth, looking to Heathrow Airport, we find out how a creative recruitment strategy helped them identify a 'new brand' of Security Officer.

Fifth, we hear about assessment associated with 'Enterprise Leadership,' using psychometrics in senior executive recruitment.

Next, the Co-op Group's Insurance business shares their experience of working with Business Psychologists to deploy a 'whole person' hiring model.

Penultimately, we have a case study from the National Health Service (NHS), demonstrating evidence-based rigour whilst pursuing assessment innovations.

The final case study in this first section brings assessment closer to home for Business Psychologists, as it describes a leading Consultancy's internal recruitment assessment approach.

The 'Good Doctor' Formula

Overview

The Psychologists' challenge concerned the future of UK health services.

Non-academic attributes, such as integrity and empathy, are essential to quality patient care; but had not been addressed in selection to medical careers.

Adding critical behavioural elements into the Clinical Aptitude Test series of assessments for medical and dental students could change that.

These Business Psychologists found a way to enable universities to identify applicants to medical and dental degrees – who were likely to lack the skills required to deliver high quality healthcare – in a reliable, validated, cost-efficient manner that supported social mobility.

Challenge

Traditionally, student selection into medicine has focused on academic attainment. However recent research has shown, to be effective, doctors require non-academic attributes as well. In fact, it has been reported that complaints about doctors often relate to a lack of these skills; and it is often when doctors lack these skills that they fail in practice.

The Work Psychology Group (WPG) recognised the opportunity this presented, to apply science to improve the situation.

The Psychologists observed that major concerns were raised in government enquiries in the preceding decade regarding a failure in "compassionate care" in UK healthcare. They felt that this verdict was worrying and highlighted the impact of staff behaviour on patient care. They believed that it was in the interest of the UK public to be clear on how to select for these types of attributes in medical admissions. They focused on how they could help to ensure that doctors have the requisite non-academic skills, like integrity and empathy, to provide quality patient care.

The Psychologists observed that medical and dental degree admissions, which form the 'gateway' to the profession, would be an ideal focus.

At the time, the University Clinical Aptitude Test (UKCAT) was the most widely accepted medical school entrance exam across universities in the UK, with tens of thousands of students taking the assessments each year. (It has since become an internationally accepted entrance exam in the selection process for medicine, and so renamed from UKCAT to UCAT.)

The UKCAT exam structure contained four sections: Verbal Reasoning, Decision Making, Quantitative Reasoning and Abstract Reasoning.

These assessments did not address domains such as Integrity, Perspective-Taking and Team Involvement, believed to be highly important in medical and dental careers. Could a solution be launched, alongside the existing cognitive tests, to assess these?

WPG wanted to create a solution which would:

- effectively predict medical and dental student performance; being valid for the selection of future doctors and dentists; and
- help to widen access to women, ethnic minorities and those from less advantaged backgrounds

Approach

In selecting the tool and approach to use, the Psychologists considered evidence for Situational Judgement Tests (SJTs) as predictors of job performance, including:

- Cleland et al., 2012
- Powis, 2014
- Francis, 2013
- Clevenger, et al., 2001
- Patterson, et al., 2012
- Patterson, et al., 2016a
- Whitla, et al., 2003

- Paez, et al., 2008
- Cohen & Steinecke, 2006

These studies suggested SJTs offer an appealing and cost-efficient solution. SJTs assess applicants' judgements in response to different situations in a specific role. Researchers agree that, when designed appropriately, SJTs can predict job performance reliably and are well-received by applicants.

They also believed that it was crucial to "widen access" in the workplace, so that more people from different backgrounds could enter the medical profession. SJTs have also been found to show smaller differences between demographic groups compared to cognitive tests. So, this could help students to develop cultural competence and make the healthcare workforce more representative of the population, which could in turn improve patient satisfaction and patient outcomes.

Tool Design

The Business Psychologists followed best practice SJT design (Patterson, et al. 2016). This process is manifold. As an overview, this included:

- Role analysis to identify evidence-based non-academic criteria
- Expert panels to identify sufficient agreement on 'correct' responses for scenarios
- Full pilot and evaluation to guide live test construction

Further, the UKCAT consortium as a stakeholder group was an academic audience. They showed keen interest in the scientific evidence underpinning selection. The Psychologists wanted to ensure the defensibility of the SJT, and this had to be demonstrably clear, so that medical and dental schools would have the confidence to actually use the SJT in practice. WPG, Pearson VUE and the UKCAT Board co-created the goals for the SJT, in order to achieve this. Goals set included:

- Psychometric reliability (consistency) to be evidenced
- Face validity, to be perceived as relevant by applicants
- Content validity to be demonstrated, focussed on the target domains
- Administration to be relatively quick
- Evidence of predictive validity to be collected

Given the ethical considerations in terms of widening access, it was especially important to the Psychologists to avoid Adverse Impact on any group wherever possible. A statistical method – 'differential item functioning' – was used on pilot data to identify items that showed bias, so these could be avoided. Thorough reviews were then conducted.

Validation Project

UKCAT consortium members were consulted and invited to participate. The study was designed collaboratively with four participating schools: three medical and one dental. This provided 223 first-year medical and dental students as participants, who had completed the first live SJT.

The Psychologists observed that an appropriate outcome measure of first year performance did not exist, so they designed one. A bespoke questionnaire was designed for tutors to complete, that assessed the same attributes as the SJT. However, this had to be meaningful. They found that tutors' feedback on an initial rating scale made it difficult to differentiate one student from another. They wanted it to be accurate, and engaging for tutors, so they used a 'relative percentile' method: an innovative approach that achieves greater range and scoring accuracy than rating students independently (Goffin, et al., 2009). Students' performance was ranked relatively, on a visual scale, in comparison to the whole year group.

Care was taken by the Psychologists to ensure that all students and tutors were briefed about the research and provided consent. It was explained that students' names would not be known or reported and that they were free to not participate or to withdraw. All materials were available to Ethics Committees to ensure transparency before sign-off. It was emphasised to all those involved that the research could have significant implications for how future UK doctors and dentists are selected, and therefore the quality of healthcare for the general UK public. This emphasis on the overarching motivation was essential in generating the interest and sample required.

Outcome

The Psychologists believe that this work has had a major impact on high-stakes selection for medical and dental admissions. The project findings successfully influenced stakeholders to implement the

UKCAT SJT as an effective, practical shortlisting method to sift applicants who are likely to struggle if selected. Their findings supported the use of more granular scores, allowing for finer distinctions to influence decision-making. They report that this has led to valuable savings for universities by reducing time and resources spent on interviewing. Importantly, the work suggests that the SJT can identify those who may impact negatively on healthcare services and patient outcomes if otherwise granted entry to the profession.

Goals achieved included:

- Psychometric reliability evidenced
    - Cronbach α=.75-.79, i.e. internal consistency reliability was within acceptable range
- Face validity
    - Perceived relevance was reported as high; just 11% of applicants disagreed with this
- Content validity was demonstrated, focussed on the target domains
- Administration was relatively quick with an average completion time of 27 minutes
    - This was achieved through innovative design format; candidates responded using a four-point scale to rate the appropriateness of options in response to scenarios. This increased the number of 'data points' collected within the testing time
- Evidence of predictive validity to be collected
    - Specifically, they found a highly favourable correlation between students' SJT scores and medical and dental school performance regarding the target attributes (N=217, corrected r=.34), which suggested that the SJT sufficiently predicted performance

Group Differences Investigation

Applicants consented to provide this information, and their scores on cognitive tests and the SJT were linked to their socio-economic status (SES), ethnicity (BME), and gender.

Regarding group differences, the Designers found that applicants' SES impacted their SJT scores (d= .13 - .20) far less than their cognitive scores (d= .38 - .35), suggesting that the SJT notably helped redress the disadvantage to lower SES applicants, as intended. Whilst this was not found for ethnicity, females scored better on the SJT than males. Hence, the addition of the SJT to the UKCAT could enhance the diversity of student intake (Lievens, et al., 2016).

The Psychologists recognized that the importance and demonstrable quality of this work had international significance, particularly in South-East Asia and Australasia where their methodology and its benefits proliferated. This furthered WPG's service to UK Medical Royal Colleges and the Medical Schools Council who adopted WPG selection recommendations as UK policy, which they reported generated significant improvements and savings for the NHS.

They decided that the research should not stop there. The Psychologists later began investigating the SJT's validity further along the training pathway, especially as research suggests SJTs become more predictive in clinical practice after medical school, when non-academic attributes become increasingly relevant (Patterson, et al., 2016a).

The Business Psychologists reported learning much from this work. The relative percentile method mitigated the common challenge with questionnaire-based validation. However, they felt that had not fully resolved 'the criterion problem.' In other words, they felt the need for a rounded picture of 'performance,' beyond tutors' views alone, to boost the evidence base. So, they began linking SJT scores with student peer reviews and exam data.

Further, they continued refining their methodology to further to minimise ethnicity differences by:

- Reducing wordiness and colloquialisms; the effect of English proficiency as a potential confounder
- Piloting different scoring techniques

These studies suggest the UCAT SJT was a valid, reliable and cost-effective way to assess non-academic attributes in medical and dental selection, whilst widening access to the profession, especially regarding social mobility. This approach was innovative, in context, whilst also rigorous and evidence-based. Their work strongly suggests that this method will help to ensure that selected doctors and dentists have the requisite skills to cope with the challenges of future professional practice, and, longer term, improvement in the overarching quality of future UK healthcare.

Acknowledgements

Stuart Martin CPsychol, Senior Consultant, WPG

Helena Edwards CPsychol, Senior Consultant, WPG

Professor Fiona Patterson, Project Director, WPG

Professor Filip Lievens, Associate Researcher, WPG

Vicki Ashworth, WPG Team

Anna Rosselli, WPG Team

Fran Cousans, WPG Team

Helen Baron, WPG Team

Sandra Nicholson, Chair of UKCAT Research Board

Rachel Greatrix, UKCAT Chief Operations Officer

The four participating medical/dental schools, who requested anonymity

An Emergency Services Emergency

Overview

The skills needed for modern firefighters has evolved significantly, with fighting fires and saving lives being only one part of a very demanding role. The need remains for them to use modern equipment to address the full range of emergencies they may face. Increasingly they are also required to effectively communicate with, engage and educate their community. Therefore, the requirements to be an effective modern firefighter are broad, yet specific, highlighting the need to have an effective recruitment strategy to support the identification of this talent.

Three Welsh Fire and Rescue Services collaborated with Business Psychology Consultants at a&dc to redesign their recruitment process in light of a large recruitment campaign for Wholetime Firefighters. They worked together to utilise a range of fair, objective and mobile optimised online tools to make the Services' recruitment accessible to a broader population.

Challenge

Fire and Rescue Services in Wales are provided by three fire and rescue authorities, covering North Wales, Mid and West Wales and South Wales (the Services). They planned to undertake a recruitment campaign at a time when the Services had not recruited any Wholetime Firefighters for three years. (Full-time or 'Wholetime Duty' Firefighters in Wales work on average 42 hours per week.) The Services were particularly concerned with ensuring the process identified the right talent to deal with the challenges of the modern fire service. And that it did so in a way that was inclusive, fair and objective.

Essentially, the Services were keen to deliver a recruitment process that utilised technology and advancements in talent assessment to address the following requirements:

- Timescales: Deliver a multi-lingual suite of online solutions within 13 weeks

- Robust and engaging: Design a process that reflects the modern Fire and Rescue realities, and identifies talent that have the skills to be effective modern firefighters
- Fair for all: The Services passionately believed that a more diverse workforce would bring benefits, such as greater innovation and creativity, and an understanding of how to serve its communities better. Therefore, it was extremely important that the assessments designed were fair to all groups
- Cost effective: It was critical that the automated solutions were used to make the process as time and cost efficient as possible

The Services chose to work with Business Psychologists at a&dc, as they had seen the benefits that Police Constabularies had in modernising their recruitment process when working with a&dc's team of Consultants. The Consultants provided stakeholders evidence of these outcomes and put them in contact with other stakeholders within the police to help them explore what it would be like to work with a&dc. The evidence-based approach, conferred by utilising Business Psychology processes, was essential in convincing the Services' internal stakeholders that the process would deliver what was required.

Approach

The approach taken on this project was focused on addressing the requirements set out by the Services. After an initial exploratory piece of work was carried out to identify the suite of online tools to be used, the project commenced.

Timescales

The project had short timescales – 13 weeks – and a delivery date that could not be moved. Typically, a project of this size and complexity would require six to eight months for the team to deliver; especially as new mobile compatible software was specifically being designed for this project, and the assessments were also required to be available in both Welsh and English.

To deliver this project, a&dc, the project sponsor and project manager for the 'all Wales recruitment campaign' needed to work closely with each other and had to be in constant communication.

To support the successful delivery, the team took these steps:

- Transparent Project Plan:

They set out a clear project plan covering every step of the design, all deliverables, resources needed, and requirements for sign off. Due to the ambitious timelines, the project plan evolved and was updated accordingly. However, due to the effective communication and hard work of both teams, all of the overarching deliverables and timescales were adhered to

- Job analysis in-situ:

   The job analysis was all carried out within Fire Stations and Training Centres, with a team of Business Psychologists in situ, interviewing staff whenever available (across nightshifts and dayshifts). This enabled a combination of job analysis and job shadowing to be carried out in very short timescales

- Proactive software implementation:

   The software was implemented in advance of having the content ready, which required much more work from the team but enabled the delivery deadlines to be met

Robust and Engaging Design

Detailed job analysis was carried out to identify the core behaviours essential for being a modern firefighter. This influenced the assessment types chosen and the features of each of the tests. An existing framework of Personal Qualities and Attributes (PQAs) was also utilised. However, as part of the design process the Consultants identified additional required behaviours that were not reflected the framework, and these were included in the suite of tests designed.

Senior management were also critical to the delivery of the project, and this buy-in was exemplified by over 300 employees being involved in the design and delivery of this project. In fact, of that 300, 50 were managers (Station Managers and Watch Managers) who were asked to be directly involved in the design and development of the suite of online tools.

The online screening process thus designed consisted of four stages, all of which were chosen to deliver a specific benefit: a candidate registration page, an interactive Realistic Job Preview (RJP), a Behaviour and Values Fit measure, and a Situational Judgement Test (SJT). To ensure that the process was available to a wider population of candidates, updates were made to the software to make the assessment components mobile compatible. Job performance data was also collected to ensure that the tests were valid and assessing performance in the role.

Fair for All

Before the assessments were implemented a review of SJT and 'fairness' literature was carried out. A review of test features – such as response type, rating scale and instructions – was also carried out to ensure the tests designed reflected best practice and incorporated learnings from previous projects.

Once designed, the tests were reviewed by a range of diversity experts to ensure they were fair and did not discriminate against any applicants. Analysis was carried out based on a representative sample and all question content with higher d-values were dropped during the design process. (Cohen suggested that d=0.2 be considered a 'small' effect size, 0.5 represents a 'medium' effect size and 0.8 a 'large' effect size. This suggests that if two groups' means do not differ by 0.2 standard deviations or more, the difference is trivial, even if it is statistically significant. See also McLeod, 2019.)

Outcome

Overall, the project was a success. The team delivered a set of multi-lingual assessments on time, despite demanding timescales, and saved over 203 working days in recruitment resources. Notably, the online suite of tools was later adopted by services across the United Kingdom, as evidence of its effectiveness.

Robust and Engaging Design

The test types designed were successfully deployed. During the design phase, 100% of Subject Matter Experts (SMEs) believed the content was fair to all groups and 96.5% said the test content was relevant. However, as with all processes and tools, constant monitoring and improvement is essential. The next year, an additional set of three Fire Service specific ability tests were added to the portfolio of online tools.

The success and quality of the assessments meant that other Fire and Rescue Services later adopted this suite of online tests. Nine other services across England started using the suite of online tests, with over 15,000 applicants going through the process in England alone. Within two years of deployment, over 30,000 applicants were assessed by this process.

Client Feedback

"The system itself was very easy to use. Our recruitment process required two members of the HR team to facilitate the online testing. Traditionally, this would have required a whole team of people to be involved in the sifting and assessment stage, which has brought huge efficiencies in our processes…I would recommend using the process to any other Fire and Rescue service who is considering recruitment of firefighters." - *County Durham & Darlington FRS*

Fair for All

Analysis of the fairness and validity of the staged process was carried out on a sample of 17,000 candidates. Based on this analysis, the Behaviour and Values Fit measure does not demonstrate any Adverse Impact for minority groups when examining gender, ethnicity, sexual orientation and age. The Situational Judgement Test did not demonstrate adverse impact for any group at the 45th percentile or below.

This analysis was the subject of several conference papers, including 'How to make Situational Judgement Tests Fairer' (British Psychological Societies' 2017 DOP Conference). This paper referenced the steps taken on this project to ensure the online tests were as fair as possible to specific minority groups.

Cost Effective Process

Three years prior, when a similar Wholetime Firefighter campaign was run, it required a much larger team of Assessors and required a total of 224 days of resources (£18,147.09) to process 2,096 application forms. This equated to £8.66 per application. This campaign required 21 days worth of resources (£2,106.58) and equated to 36p per application. Use of the tools provided an estimated saving of £49,000 in staffing costs because there was no manual assessing or inputting.

"If processed in the same way as in [the past] it would have taken up an enormous amount of resources, which we could ill afford in these days of budget cuts... the cost for the initial sifting was a 65% reduction in cost." – *Devon & Somerset FRS*

Acknowledgements

Mary Mescal, a&dc

Ali Shalfrooshan, a&dc

Gillian Goss, HR Manager, South Wales Fire and Rescue Service

Tim Jackson, Sales and Marketing Director, Fire Service College

Banking on Values

Overview

Banks depend on customers to have a great deal of trust in them. And yet commentators suggest 2008 marked the year when 'almost the entire world lost faith in the ethics and integrity of banks.' Most banks have worked hard to regain public trust whilst facing increased competition, opportunity and challenges as a result of the fintech revolution.

Whilst addressing those big issues, along with the media scrutiny and financial challenges they brought, The Royal Bank of Scotland (RBS) was continuing to invest in attracting and recruiting top talent. They worked with Business Psychology Consultants at the Work Psychology Group (WPG) to address their demands for top talent who would support their agenda to embed and sustain the Bank's cultural values.

Challenge

Many observed that the global recession cast a spotlight over the culture of banking. Short-term thinking and inadequate risk control had created issues (Kandola, et al., 2013). In response, RBS created a multi-year plan with the objective of becoming 'number one for customer service, trust and advocacy by 2020.' The Bank worked to ensure that customer care principles – such as building trust, risk control and ethical decision-making – were more explicit than ever.

The bank wanted their values to resonate through the thousands of interactions they had with their customers every day. In this context RBS wanted to attract and recruit applicants who possessed the attributes that best complemented their values and strategic goals for customer advocacy.

RBS had also publicly committed to achieving a fully 50/50 gender-balanced workforce by 2030. And they wanted to increase recruitment from less advantaged backgrounds. This priority linked to the Bank's value of 'Doing the Right Thing,' including recognising the case for diversity (Slater et al., 2008).

'RBS Early Career,' the team dedicated to recruiting Graduates and Apprentices, sought a solution to embed the Bank's values within selection criteria, and the overall candidate experience. Indicators for success established by the team were psychometric considerations of reliability, validity and fairness, and a demonstrable shift in 'pass ratios' particularly for women and those who went to state schools as opposed to independent schools.

Approach

The Bank's values, to be incorporated in the recruitment process, were:

- Serving Customers
- Working Together
- Thinking Long Term
- Doing the Right Thing

Identifying Issues

The Psychologists evaluated data from 4,628 RBS candidates. An important finding concerned the initial candidate filter, a 'motivational questionnaire.' Higher pass rates were observed at this stage for males, and those from independent schools, compared with females and candidates from state schools. These differences did not appear to link to performance at subsequent assessment stages.

Other options were considered, to achieve ambitious gender balance targets and widen participation to those from less advantaged backgrounds. For example, the Psychologists demonstrated that traditional high-volume selection methods, such as cognitive tests and A-levels, were becoming increasingly incongruent with the social mobility agenda, and links between career success and UCAS points remained unclear (Kirkup, et al., 2008). (The Universities and Colleges Admissions Service in the UK (UCAS) uses point to measure the relative value of all post-16 qualifications in the UK.)

RBS wanted to introduce changes to improve their process accordingly.

A bespoke Situational Judgement Test (SJT) was considered a more suitable solution.

Applying Science

In advising the client on the use of this form of assessment, a range of factors were considered including:

- SJT literature demonstrates favourable candidate reactions (Chan & Schmitt, 2002) and face validity (Clevenger, et al., 2001)
- SJT validation shows good reliability (consistency), predictive validity (McDaniel, et al., 2007), and incremental validity over cognitive (Koczwara, et al., 2012) and personality measures (Patterson, et al., 2009), i.e. they can add value by predicting job performance even when cognitive ability and personality data are controlled for
- SJT assessments often show reduced Adverse Impact over cognitive tests (Lievens, Buyse & Sackett, 2005), such as smaller group differences between, for example, males and females

This evidence was highly attractive to RBS to address their priorities and ensure rigour in the selection process.

Project Steps

A test specification was developed collaboratively with RBS stakeholders. Because the population was Graduates with limited work experience, from diverse backgrounds, the SJT was designed to assess core Values rather than job knowledge, and present realistic dilemmas that could be faced in the role. A short 20-minute test was designed, to avoid over-burdening candidates. Scenarios were reviewed according to RBS's 'Writing Simply' campaign, fairness of topics, content validity, and to avoid RBS-specific knowledge. The item development process included:

- Interviews with subject matter experts (SMEs) to generate content
  - Scenario development interviews were held with a range of personnel including Graduate Programme leaders, Hiring and Resourcing Managers, and key change agents supporting the 2020 ambition, such as Culture and Enterprise Risk. This ensured that the SJT contexts were varied and representative, and that stakeholders influenced content directly
- Focus groups with SMEs and incumbents to review draft scenarios to ensure they were relevant
  - Stakeholder focus groups shaped the content, informed by the Bank's values and an existing performance framework to ensure content validity
- Scoring keys determined by SME consensus
  - SMEs discussed in detail correct keys, using RBS Values to guide agreement. This included the Bank's 'Yes' checklist to ensure appropriateness. When considering responses the group asked, for example: 'Will this decision keep our customers' assets safe?'

Content was rejected at this stage if there was insufficient agreement. This ensured that keys were anchored firmly in the criteria and Values

- SJT piloting was completed by RBS incumbent Graduates (n=127)
- Items were rejected if they correlated poorly with other items, and if they did not differentiate between candidates, such as by being too easy or difficult
- Final content and scoring keys were ratified with stakeholders and showed good internal consistency reliability (Cronbach α=.82) and that the test was differentiating between candidates sufficiently

Below is an example SJT scenario with response options:

You've been working on a new RBS product called SimpleBank that will improve the way customers do their banking online. You have just given a presentation to other departments to inform colleagues of the product and its benefits to customers. John, who works in another department, approaches you. He disagrees with many of the points from your presentation. You disagree with what he is saying.

How appropriate are each of the following responses in this situation?

A) Inform John politely that you do not appreciate being spoken to in this way

B) Politely challenge John's criticism, using the knowledge you have gained from working on the presentation

C) Ask John more about why he disagreed with many of the points from your presentation

Outcome

Reliable and Fair

Analysis was undertaken to establish the validity of the tool with a large candidate sample (n=16,339):

- A 'pass mark' was established to filter out 30% of candidates with no Adverse Impact on any demographic sub-group investigated (using the four-fifths rule), including between Black and Minority Ethnic (BME) and White candidates

- Data showed a higher pass ratio of female applicants compared to male
- A t-test showed that females were outperforming males on the SJT to a statistically significant extent ($p<.001$). Further, the same relationship was found for candidates who went to non-selective state schools, compared to independent schools ($p<.01$). Reassuringly however, neither of these differences showed Adverse Impact for any group
- Criterion validity (i.e., is the SJT measuring what we intend it to be measuring?) was undertaken with comparison between candidate SJT scores and subsequent interview scores. A statistically significant positive correlation was found (N=820, $r=.14$, $p<.01$), providing evidence of criterion validity, unlike the preceding motivational questionnaire

Feedback

The Psychologists found stakeholder feedback to be consistently positive. The Assessment Centre pass criteria were raised accordingly to reflect the improved standard of candidates. Hiring managers' time spent interviewing was reduced. The approach generated great interest across other contexts, such as Volume Hiring and Apprenticeships, who began implementing SJT's to support specific objectives.

Additionally, candidates' feedback was highly positive and, importantly, candidate tracking data pre- and post-SJT implementation showed that candidate attrition rate reduced notably. And the test-taking experience became 50% quicker.

Monitoring

The level of challenge presented by the SJT continued to be monitored. Whilst differentiating effectively, there was opportunity to increase the difficulty of the assessment to enable a more efficient, larger filter. The Bank later trialled a blended approach of item types, to ensure that a sufficient degree of challenge remained over time.

In summary, the Psychologists believe that the evidence gathered demonstrated that the RBS Graduate SJT met robust psychometric criteria in terms of reliability and some sources of validity evidence. This meant that the SJT could be used defensibly as a selection tool to assess for the Bank's desired competencies and Values. Further, it could do so without creating Adverse Impact on any demographic group. Ultimately, this enhanced the way in which the Bank could achieve its specific aims around embedding the behaviours and Values required in its people to support the 2020 objective, widen access to banking careers to minority groups, and achieve a 50/50 gender balance by 2030.

Acknowledgements

Stuart Martin CPsychol, Senior Consultant, WPG

Dr Anna Koczwara CPsychol, Leadership and Organisational Capability, RBS

Glen McGowan, Head of Early Career, RBS

Louisa Hayman, Early Career Team, RBS

Securing Every Journey

Overview

Airport security is something many travellers may take for granted, but it takes significant work behind the scenes to ensure it. Few travellers are even aware that half of an airport's workforce may be Security Officers.

London serves as the largest aviation hub in the world by passenger traffic, and London's Heathrow airport is the largest airport in the UK, typically handling over 80 million international passengers annually. Heathrow has always paid close attention to effective recruitment of Security Officers. And, when they recognised an opportunity to develop a greater culture of customer service, they looked to this community too.

This case study recounts how Heathrow introduced a creative and novel recruitment strategy to help them identify a 'new brand' of Security Officers who could demonstrate the aptitude and the behaviours to do this critically important role.

Challenge

Getting the recruitment strategy right for the vital role of Security Officer at Heathrow Airport is imperative. Traditionally, Security Officers were recruited for their technical skills such as vigilance and observation. Many came from the police or armed services, bringing a natural sense of authority and discipline. Whilst these skills were still vitally important, Heathrow wanted to develop a greater culture of customer service. So, they needed to find ways to recruit candidates from more diverse backgrounds who would also possess the customer service characteristics desired.

The Heathrow Talent team set themselves a goal of creating an innovative and engaging recruitment process that would promote the Heathrow brand, and help them to identify a new cohort of Security Officers who would help them to fulfil their vision of "Making every journey better."

The recruitment strategy addressed six clear ambitions, which provided a brief for the design of the recruitment process:

- Increase the quality of candidates

- Identify individuals who have a strong customer focus whilst maintaining the security of passengers
- Showcase the role
  - Use techniques which showcase the role of Security Officer whilst ensuring candidates are aware of the what the role will involve
- Engage the candidates
  - Use innovative methods to promote their employee value proposition and gain candidate engagement, appealing to both millennial talent and more experienced, potentially older hires
- Ensure fairness, diversity and inclusion
  - Continue to address their diversity and inclusion agenda by attracting and assessing across genders, generations, and ethnicities, providing everyone with equal opportunity
- Streamline the recruitment process
  - Make the recruitment process more efficient to improve recruiter experience
- Evolve the Heathrow brand
  - Build and leverage the community and employer brand, by demonstrating strong commitment to the local community, and recognising that candidates (successful or unsuccessful) may also be their passengers

Approach

Heathrow decided to partner with Business Psychology Consultants and Assessment Specialists at Saville Assessment (Saville) on this project. Together they developed an innovative, multi-faceted and tailored multimedia assessment experience. Key stakeholders from across the business were involved in the design of the assessment which was constantly reviewed against the organisation's strategic objectives.

Improving Candidate Quality

Security Officer candidates were offered a realistic preview of the roles, showcasing the opportunities, challenges and environment they would be working within if successful in their application. This allowed for proactive self-selection by candidates, prior to application.

When individuals applied, it was important to assess both the behavioural potential of the candidate and their technical ability to do the job.

The innovative new assessment, which was designed as a bespoke tool, involved two separate elements:

– A situational judgement style assessment to establish whether applicants had the behavioural characteristics they were looking for in their Security Officers; this was mapped to Heathrow's Security Officer competency framework and focused particularly on providing passengers with an exceptional customer experience

– A visual assessment which measured an applicant's ability to 'check' and identify differences between two images presented on screen. This was an early indicator for the mental agility required to work with Heathrow's security scanning equipment

Showcase the Role

These two assessments were blended to form a unique and dynamic assessment experience. By doing this, they hoped to ensure that the candidate experience started in a positive way and provided a truly realistic preview to the role, with strong branding throughout to reinforce the brand identity of Heathrow.

Engage the Candidates

Generally, applicants prefer selection tools which they perceive as job related. Saville research on applicant reactions to situation-based assessments showed that they were perceived favourably; multimedia formats, such as video-based assessments, resulted in even more positive perceptions than written formats. On this basis, Heathrow chose to use a multimedia assessment.

Ensure Fairness, Diversity and Inclusion

The team understood that situation-based assessments offer a fair and legally defensible approach to selection, as they typically have lower levels of Adverse Impact, by age, gender and ethnicity.

Additionally, features of the assessments were designed to enhance the accessibility of the assessment, including:

– Replaying scenarios
– Providing subtitles
– Text being clearly legible on all screens

The assessment gave two scores, one linking to the scenario-based element and one for the visual checking element. This enabled the recruiting team to quickly and efficiently make informed decisions.

In addition to an engaging selection process, the team wanted to make sure that they were continuing to reflect their Employee Value Proposition (EVP) and commitment to the community in the feedback provided to applicants as well.

They worked with Saville to develop tailored candidate feedback reports which would be made available to all applicants, after the first stage of the assessment process, whether successful or unsuccessful. Feedback reports were sent automatically via the online assessment platform, so this placed no additional administrative burden on Heathrow Recruiters.

These reports provided an opportunity for candidates to understand their behavioural style within the workplace. The reports provided advice on how to leverage their strengths when going for interview, or if applying for different roles. In addition, they advised unsuccessful applicants of other opportunities that were available at Heathrow, which they may be interested in applying for.

If successful, applicants were invited to a telephone interview. The telephone interview assessed applicants against Heathrow's competency framework, as well as a question which explored each applicant's motivation for the role.

The team also redesigned the Assessment Centre material to ensure it was aligned to their strategic objectives. Specifically, they created two exercises that prioritised customer service, whilst balancing other elements of the security triangle. Each of the scenarios mimicked the types of scenarios that Heathrow Security Officers experience, providing a "day in the life" feel to the Assessment Centre, continuing the realistic job preview. All materials were designed to be visually appealing and showcase Heathrow's strong branding.

Outcome

Increased Quality of Candidates

These efforts effectively increased the quality of the candidates reaching later stages of the assessment process. Analysis revealed that the multimedia assessment exercise positively predicted how applicants would do in the later stages of the selection process (=.27). In particular, they were able to predict applicants who would perform well on subsequent measures of customer focus, a high priority for the team.

Showcased the Role

The assessment was seen, by applicants, to provide a realistic preview of the type of situations they would likely find themselves in, giving them a greater insight into the requirements of the role. One candidate stated, "I enjoyed taking this assessment as it seemed very realistic to the types of situations I look forward to dealing with."

Engaged Candidates

The Heathrow multimedia assessment had higher completion rates than the previous assessment tool. Candidate feedback to the assessment was positive with one candidate stating: "I actually enjoyed this exercise. Probably the most fun exercise I have carried out online." Feedback from the resourcing team went onto explain that "it seems a much more user-friendly process, which is great." They also found that the assessment was completed successfully across different generations.

Fairness, Diversity and Inclusion

When analysing results of the assessment to check for Adverse Impact and to ensure fairness, it was found that the multimedia assessment experience met the conditions of the four-fifths rule for gender, ethnicity and age.

They found that applicants across a broad range of ages were completing the assessment – aged between 16 and 65 years – as well as different ethnicities. Assessment completions were made by people of Chinese, Bangladeshi, Indian, Pakistani, Black African, Black American, Black Caribbean, Arabic, Turkish, White British, White Gypsy or Irish Traveller and White Irish ethnicities.

A Streamlined Recruitment Process

Following the introduction of the multimedia assessment exercise, the team introduced specific assessment score cut-offs which provided them with the potential to schedule 690 less telephone interviews and 117 less Assessment Centres per cohort, with a saving of approximately £40,000 to the business for each cohort.

An Evolved Brand

In addition to providing an innovative and highly branded multi-media assessment experience, tens of thousands of feedback reports have been sent to applicants following completion of the assessment. These reports provide tangible and usable feedback to both successful and unsuccessful applicants as well as information on other roles available at Heathrow.

Acknowledgements

Danni Clements, Managing Consultant, Saville Assessment

Rab McIver, R&D Director, Saville Assessment

Jake Smith, Senior Researcher, Saville Assessment

Jack Andrews, Emerging Talent Manager, Heathrow

Enterprise Leader Selection

Overview

Nationwide Building Society elected to bring their previously outsourced executive selection process in-house, in line with their focus on increasing efficiency. They created an 'Enterprise Leadership' assessment solution, using psychometric assessment, for senior executive recruitment.

The approach was designed to provide a context-rich understanding of their leadership population, embed research findings in their processes and enable analysis of their leadership capability and pipeline with validated internal and external benchmarks. This work was supported by Nationwide's psychometric partners at SHL.

Challenge

Nationwide commenced this work with a requirement to:

- Align their assessment strategy across the organisation with their business strategy, most importantly at senior executive level

  The arrival of their new CEO in 2016 provided a clearer and more defined purpose for the Society, and gave them a much-needed platform to work from. Research published by the Corporate Research Forum (CRF) bore out the importance of having a strong link between performance measurement and business strategy

- Focus on efficiency: was the Society making the best use of their members' money?

  As a mutual organisation they must justify everything they spend, and it seemed right to challenge the use of external psychologists for executive assessment when the Society had people internally with the qualifications and expertise needed

- Build their understanding of the leadership capabilities needed to keep Nationwide operating for another 150 years

  This was a twofold process:

  - Identifying the capabilities needed, which they did using research from CEB and KornFerry Hay Group

- Measuring their leadership population against the capabilities needed, including establishing an external benchmark

They were clear that whatever solution they designed needed to balance their requirements around quality, cost and resources. The Leadership Development team established their design principles:

- Assess behavioural preferences and potential
- Embrace best practice
- Seek assessment synergies
- Apply appropriate benchmarks
- Optimise use (test once, multi-purpose during appropriate validity periods)
- Carry out consistent analysis

Having established these principles, they were then able to engage with their internal and external stakeholders. Their primary partners in developing the Enterprise Leadership approach were SHL. Nationwide and SHL had a long history of working together; they had jointly developed a model of potential underpinned by psychometric assessment which had been validated over the previous five years and was at the heart of their Enterprise Leadership process. (Nationwide reference "Enterprise Leadership." Enterprise Leadership is usually referenced as an approach for encouraging leaders to focus on organisational outcomes, working on behalf of the whole organisation, rather than only focusing on their own business unit or team. Their partners at SHL suggest: "Leaders are navigating increasingly complex organisations and expectations are higher than ever… But leaders with the most impact are not just solid individual performers; they take a broader view to deliver stronger business performance as a collective. We call this Enterprise Leadership.")

Internally the Leadership Development team worked closely with their colleagues in Executive Resourcing to determine the potential demand for the service and potential value add of bringing the process in-house. Once they had gained their support and identified the value add (financial savings and improved candidate experience) they were able to gain support more widely from the People and Culture senior leadership team within Nationwide, including the Executive Director.

The project team made a commitment to:

- Provide and add selection insight of equal quality to that previously delivered by external suppliers
- Provide year on year cost saving of £170K
- Add developmental support into the process for new hire Executives, once onboarded

Approach

Setting Criteria

The areas of focus for Nationwide reflected CEB's global Enterprise Leadership research:

- Connected strategies
- Cross-function coordination prioritised
- Strategic alignment of resources
- Talent viewed as a corporate asset

Working with SHL, Nationwide designed a blend of assessments which gave them both indications of performance and potential, a role-specific and enterprise-wide view with an external benchmark.

Nationwide selected, for focus:

- Job fit assessment, mapped to Nationwide's competency framework
- Enterprise assessments, providing a view of the most critical enterprise traits (Sustainable, Agile, Connected)
- Conduct assessment, accounting for increased regulation emphasising fair customer outcomes. These elements were also mapped into their competency framework, so they knew which competencies were most critical for senior leaders to meet these obligations
- Potential assessment, combining their framework and assessments as a basis of their High Potential (HiPo) model, in place since 2013 and therefore able to provide a measure consistent with their internal benchmark

Assessments Selected

Nationwide chose to use a combination of three assessments in the Enterprise Leadership process:

- Occupational Personality Questionnaire (OPQ)

Personality inventories explore preferred ways of working and more broadly how you relate to people, how you like to think and your emotional style; OPQ dimensions are mapped to assess individuals' preferences and how they might impact on behaviour

- Motivation Questionnaire

Dimensions are mapped to individual's motivations and how they might impact on drive and motivation for certain aspects of work; this offers insight in terms of how willing, rather than how able, an individual may be to do something

- Inductive Reasoning

This assessment evaluates the individual's capacity to solve novel problems, work flexibly with unfamiliar information, and deal with complexity when new information is presented to them. People who perform well on these tests tend to have a greater capacity to think conceptually as well as analytically

Nationwide brought assessments upfront in the selection process, rather than the more typical trend of being used to validate a decision already made. These were positioned as giving managers insight and information so that they could be more confident in, and accountable for, these critical people decisions. This was quite a shift from the expectation that the assessment would provide the answer.

Outputs

Measuring Enterprise Leadership means they can see if candidates are 'fit for the future' (linked to research intelligence and Nationwide strategy). Decision-makers have insights earlier in the selection process enabling them to be more confident in and accountable for critical people decisions; and they provide feedback to all candidates regardless of outcome.

The assessments were used to produce a suite of reports:

- Enterprise Leadership Insights – drawn from the OPQ and used at first stage interview by the Hiring Manager and resourcing manager looking at suitability for the specific role
- Enterprise Leadership Potential – drawn from all three and used at second stage interview by a psychometric specialist looking at potential for the future

- Enterprise Leadership Feedback – drawn from all three and used by psychometric specialists to inform development if appointed, or development of unsuccessful internal candidates
- Enterprise Leadership Personal Insights – self interpreted report drawn from all three if taken, provided to unsuccessful external candidates

As the assessment results had a 24-month validity period, Nationwide used the content beyond the hiring process; they designed the process and reports to support primarily selection, but also development conversations. They ensured all candidates received assessment feedback with a suite of reports designed to achieve this. Successful candidates received feedback, development planning and support from an internal coach/mentor.

Outcome

Savings Achieved

Nationwide achieved a significant efficiency saving, meeting their commitment to deliver year on year savings of £170K. Recruitment for their senior executive population increased over the period however, so in reality they could be said to have achieved greater savings.

Stakeholder Feedback

Hiring managers showed a real interest in the psychology underpinning selection and a weighing up of similarities and differences between candidates depending on the role now and future succession.

Managers remarked that it was interesting to see, in the person before them, a reflection of what they saw in the reports. Rich three-way conversations began to pervade selection decisions, between the Hiring Manager, executive resourcing and the Assessor. Most powerfully, managers remarked on feeling supported not only in their decisions but also in enabling an immediate link into development support from the wider leadership team.

A member of Nationwide's Human Resources (HR) community commented "I love the reports, it's so easy to probe really interesting areas." Conversation was stimulated at their Executive Committee, particularly around the onboarding support available to new appointments – a psychometric feedback session and up to two further sessions to explore impact in the workplace.

Approaching two years after the launch of this new approach, Nationwide were able to analyse their people to put forward internal candidates for roles based on what they knew of them. Their understanding of what capability they had internally, the capabilities they could develop, and what capabilities they may need to source externally had been refined. They had a better view of their peoples' performance and potential, and career aspiration in context. They had greater insight to how individuals could be successful and contribute most effectively to Nationwide's success.

Validation Findings

Their annual validation activity in conjunction with SHL highlighted that those with a stronger 'fit' to their Enterprise Leadership assessment were stronger performers once in the business. They also identified that the clusters linked to 'sustainable' and 'agile' were most closely linked to success. Their performance compared to the external benchmark was pleasing too – with Nationwide above the benchmark in seven of twelve behaviours in the competency framework.

For Nationwide, the data and insights tell a compelling story. They report that Enterprise Leadership gives them a view of the 'whole person,' for things going well and potential behavioural challenges. It delivered what they had expected it to, against their original objectives of quality, efficiency, resource and candidate experience.

Acknowledgements

Julie Foster, Leadership Development Manager, Nationwide Building Society

SHL, with special thanks to Chris Martin and Andy Partington

Whole Person Hiring

Overview

Co-op Group in the UK can trace its roots to the co-operative consumer societies established by the Rochdale Pioneers. The Co-operative Insurance Company was launched in 1867 to provide fire insurance for co-operative societies. Now, as part of the Co-op Group, it is a consumer co-operative owned by millions of members.

Like many organisations, they faced challenges in optimising their Sales Advisor recruitment process. Their filtering criteria appeared to be costing them some good candidates, and yet the time and effort required to improve their approach seemed unsustainable.

In this case study, Business Psychologists at TMP (a PeopleScout Company) worked with Co-op Insurance to re-design their assessment process for Sales Advisors. They applied the TMP 'whole person' model which suggests that assessing capability, passion, purpose, mindset, balance and results, in context, offers the power to predict performance.

Challenge

Co-op Insurance identified challenges in their recruitment process for Sales Advisors, including:

- Manual sifting was proving resource-intensive, consuming significant amounts of the Resourcing team's time required to review hundreds of Curricula Vitae (CVs)
- CV sifting appeared to be suboptimal
  - Candidates may report contact centre or insurance experience, and thus be progressed in the process, but then not necessarily demonstrate the right behaviours
  - Candidates were being excluded due to a lack of relevant experience which meant overlooking some who may have had potential to succeed in these roles
- Telephone interviews were not optimised, focused largely on eligibility to work in the UK
- Quality of hire issues were being experienced, with performance issues observed amongst previous cohorts

- Time to hire, from application to appointment, was longer than desired
- Early attrition figures were higher than desired, as some incumbents demonstrated a lack of understanding of what the day-to-day role involved

The Consultants explored and uncovered what the root issues were, and summarised the two requirements as follows:

- Greater clarity in what good looked like, and therefore what was being measured
- Greater efficiency in terms of how candidates were assessed

The TMP team took a consultative approach to their work with Co-op. They ran engagement workshops with Human Resources (HR), Resourcing, Learning and Development team and operational business managers. The workshops allowed TMP to understand the challenges each stakeholder group faced, what they felt was missing from the existing process and what they wanted to see in future. They also conducted job analysis activity with incumbents, managers, and visionary stakeholders.

Through this process they understood the improvements the stakeholders would like to see. And they refined the assessment criteria to be applied. For example, they identified that candidate experience was not at all important, although it was what the existing process was predominantly based on. Further, they gained an accurate understanding of qualities which did contribute to success.

Approach

The Practitioners worked with Resourcing to understand how technology could provide an easier, quicker and more effective way of assessing the qualities required in the role. They selected to use a Tazio solution to provide candidates with an engaging experience. (See www.tazio.co.uk for details of this supplier's services.)

TMP then proposed designing a bespoke, cost-effective sifting tool, which would save Resourcing team time and help them identify candidates with the potential to develop and excel, whilst providing the candidates with a realistic preview of the role.

They proposed building this solution using their "whole person" approach to assessment. This approach assesses the 'whole person' by capturing Capability (i.e. ability), Results (i.e. experience), Behaviours, Mindset, Passion, and Purpose, thereby aiming to improve the overall predictive power of selection.

The Practitioners found that standard assessments focus solely on Capability, Results and Behaviour; predictors of performance. General mental ability (i.e. capability) is one of the most valid predictors of future performance (Schmidt & Hunter, 2004); previous experience (i.e. results) predicts job performance (Weisner & Cronshaw, 1988); and observed behaviours predict job performance ratings (Schmitt, et al, 1984).

However, in today's often unpredictable environments, they believed that assessing Purpose, Passion and Mindset provided a more comprehensive, incrementally beneficial assessment, leading to a greater predictive power in ever-changing organisations. This holistic model was influenced by the work of Carol Dweck (Dweck, 2015), Daniel Pink (Pink, 2009) and Simon Sinek (Sinek, 2016).

The Co-op's existing assessment process assessed candidates' Capability and Results (i.e. their existing experience), but did not assess Passion, Purpose or Mindset.

The TMP team applied their model to the new end-to-end process for the Co-op, designing the assessment tools from their collaborative engagement activities with stakeholders. The outputs included a realistic job preview, "one experience" sifting tool and face to face Assessment Centre.

"One Experience"

The "one experience" sifting tool replaced the initial CV sifting stage. This was an automated seamless candidate experience, combining a Situational Judgement Test (SJT), error checking test and video interview. CV sifting was removed so there was less reliance on experience only, rather assessing the whole person and progressing candidates who had great potential to succeed in these roles. Video interviews were also included in the tool, assessing passion and motivation for the business.

The SJT elements measured individuals with the right behaviours and mindset, whilst also providing a realistic job preview, in turn reducing attrition. SJTs are also found to be a valid predictor of job performance, hence improving performance once in the role (McDaniel, et al, 2001).

All elements of the "one experience" tool were designed to be completed by candidates in one sitting, reducing time to hire.

The tool consisted of:

- Image-based SJT items, realistic to the role, designed to assess Behaviour and Mindset (Dweck, 2015)
- Audio-based error-checking items, giving candidates an understanding of the situations they might face, assessing Capability
- Video interview questions assessed Purpose (Sinek, 2016), Passion (Pink, 2009) and Mindset (Dweck, 2015)

Project Management

The project was carefully managed to ensure the timescales were adhered to.

An initial kick-off meeting was conducted to clearly highlight to the client what input and resource was needed from them. Clear milestones were also identified, such as key review and sign-off points, as well as what resource was needed for the design of the SJT and error checking test.

The Consultants worked with the client to explore the best way to trial the SJT and error checking test (in which a high volume of incumbents would be needed to validate the tool in its development). Weekly project calls were conducted to engage with the client and keep them up to date on key deliverables, risks and assumptions. The high-level project plan was shared with the client, to emphasise when key deliverables would be completed.

A flexible approach to project management was applied throughout the project. For example, there were difficulties in obtaining enough incumbent completions for the tool validation, so they worked openly with the client to resolve.

Outcome

An ongoing evaluation was built into the project plan following go-live, to evaluate the effectiveness of the intervention, focusing on the following measurement criteria:

- Candidate feedback
- Assessor feedback
- Quality of candidates at Assessment Centre

Following the implementation of the tool, another stakeholder engagement meeting was conducted to obtain an evaluation of the assessment tool. Qualitative client feedback was extremely positive:

- The Resourcing team were delighted with the automation and ease of the system; they expressed that the system was easy to use and it freed up their valuable time to dedicate resource to other projects, rather than constant assessing of CVs
- The candidate feedback was positive, with candidates saying how useful it was to obtain a realistic preview of the role prior to Assessment Centre; this allowed a two-way informative process meaning candidates could self-select out of the process if they didn't feel it was right for them
- Quality at Assessment Centres increased significantly
- Time to hire was significantly reduced as candidates completed all elements of the test in one sitting
- Candidates who would previously have been overlooked due to their lack of experience progressed through to subsequent stages, some of them becoming top performers in the department

Predictive validity data for the assessment will be delivered to the client. Early indications however demonstrated that the tool was significantly impacting the recruitment process:

- Completion rate of the online assessment was 65%, suggesting less motivated candidates may not persist to completion of the assessment
- The benchmark set for the assessment progressed 50% of candidates in the process
- The success rate at Assessment Centre stage increased to 73%, from the previous pass rate which was 41%
- Anecdotally, stakeholders reported new hires from the revised process were motivated to succeed in their roles, with a

propensity for learning and a growth mindset, genuinely enjoying their day to day role

Altogether, the three elements of the "one experience" sifting tool combined meant that the tool was not only able to reduce resource consumption, time consumption for employees and applicants, but also identify talent regardless of experience, enabling a wider range of people to find a career they enjoyed and were motivated to succeed at.

Acknowledgements

The Co-operative Insurance

TMP

Evidence-Based Innovation

Overview

Maintaining rigour in any scientific endeavour, while pursuing innovation, can be challenging. There is a requirement to evidence the effectiveness of an approach, which can limit opportunities to benefit from new approaches. The answer to this dilemma lies in evidence-based innovation. Research and evidence can contribute to successful innovation and new ways of working.

This is what the largest employer in the United Kingdom, the National Health Service (NHS), elected to do. They wanted to introduce a new approach in their assessment process for the NHS Graduate Management Trainee Scheme. So, they partnered with Business Psychologists from TMP (a PeopleScout Company), who helped them ensure evidence-based rigour as they replaced first stage telephone interviews with video interviews.

Challenge

The recruitment team, for the NHS Graduate Management Trainee Scheme, take candidate experience very seriously. They recognise that they represent an organisation that the UK public is deeply and emotionally connected to. As the UK's largest employer, their scheme typically receives over 16,000 applications each year. And, since its launch in 2003, the NHS has maintained a top ten position in the Times Top 100 Graduate Employers list.

The NHS wanted to replace the telephone interview with a video interview to support their organisational objectives. Both TMP and the NHS were mindful that video interviews were still a relatively new assessment methodology and several stakeholders had concerns about the candidate reactions to the method. Therefore, as part of the objectives of introducing the video interview into the process, providing a positive candidate experience was a priority.

Setting Standards

TMP had already partnered with the NHS for the previous four years to design and deliver their graduate selection process. TMP had previously been involved in designing and implementing the telephone interview assessment at the first stage of the process. So, they were a natural choice of partner for the NHS as they decided to explore the introduction of video interviews in the context of high-volume Graduate Selection.

The existing relationship offered the Business Psychologists an opportunity to utilise multiple sources of data during this project, taking an evidence-based approach (Briner & Rousseau, 2011), to ensure a defensible result. They also fully understood the project challenges, stakeholders' values and concerns, scientific literature, organisational data and practitioner experience to consider.

Setting Objectives

The business objectives and outcomes they were aiming to achieve were:

- To provide a positive candidate experience of the video interview:

    There were concerns from stakeholders and practitioners about candidate perceptions of and satisfaction with the process. This is in line with the literature, in which candidates experience an impersonal feeling and preference for other assessment methods (Guchait, et al., 2014). As such, it was critical to design a video interview process that would mitigate these concerns and provide a positive candidate experience

- To design a video interview to predict effective performance against the NHS leadership framework:

    The assessment needed to predict future potential to perform and differentiate the highest performers as measured against the leadership behaviours

- To ensure the video Interview maintains a fair assessment approach:

    NHS were committed to ensuring that social status or other characteristics were no barrier to the best career opportunities. TMP practitioner perceptions were that the structured and flexible method would support a diverse pool of candidates and reduce bias in the process (Guchait, et al., 2014)

- For the video interview to enable recruitment process efficiencies to be made:

    NHS were looking to reduce the resource involved with scheduling and conducting telephone interviews

Approach

The Consultants believed it was important to provide a positive candidate experience of the video interview. They relied on scientific literature to inform them.

- Candidate attitudes towards new technology have been found to be significantly more positive when it is easy to use and follow, as well as when it is perceived as useful (Brenner, et al., 2016)
- Building on Social Identity theory (Tajfel, 1974), candidates are also likely to be more engaged in the selection process for organisations with whom they feel a sense of belonging
- An awareness of, and alignment with, the values and goals of the organisation will likely increase effectiveness of selection methods (Chapman & Mayers, 2015)
- Following social exchange theory, perceptions of trust will impact candidate commitment to the process and ultimately employee commitment to the organisation (Torres & Mejia, 2017)

Influenced by the above, the following features were included in the design of the video interview, and related candidate materials, to allow candidates to perform their best and engage with the process:

- Emphasis on what the video interview had been designed to assess
- Link to and recommendation to review 'our story' video on NHS careers site, explaining the values and purpose of the organisation, introducing a more personal component
- Detailed tips and guidance on what to expect and how to prepare

The Consultants needed to design a video interview to predict effective performance against the NHS leadership framework. They found that taking a multi-method assessment approach can increase predictive validity over a single measure and interview question validity. Past behaviour can also be used as a predictor of future performance (Torres & Mejia, 2017, Anderson & Cunningham-Senell, 2000, Arnold, 2005).

Informed by the above, the video interview was designed as part of a wider multi-method assessment approach to assess each area of the NHS leadership framework multiple times. The video interview included motivational and competency-based questions. Prompts were included as part of the question design to help the candidates focus their responses against the assessment criteria as, due to the nature of the interview, there would be no opportunity for probing questions.

To ensure the video interview was fair, a structured interview design was chosen. Structured interviews show increased validity in selecting individuals over semi-structured and more informal methods of assessment. Consistency across interviews and objective evaluation criteria support fairness in the process and help reduce Adverse Impact (Arnold & Randall, 2010, Blackman, 2017). In addition to the structured nature of the questions themselves, robust and objective rating criteria was included.

Regarding improved recruitment efficiencies, this method could bring a faster pace to the process, offering more control of the process, becoming easier to manage with higher flexibility in scheduling, and Interviewers spending less time assessing, which saves expense (Guchait, et al., 2014, Seans, et al., 2013, Stone, et al., 2013, Torres and Mejia, 2017, Toldi, 2011).

Project Execution

The project was carefully managed to ensure the timescales were adhered to.

An initial kick-off meeting was conducted to clearly highlight to the client what input and resources would be needed from them. Clear milestones were also identified, such as key review and sign-off points. The Consultants worked with the client to explore the best way to introduce the recommended features of the video interview design and evaluate its success in comparison with previous years when a telephone interview was used. This involved ensuring the candidate survey questions would allow for comparison with data from previous years. Comparing year-on-year data would highlight changes which could be attributed specifically to the video interview design features introduced.

The team adopted a fully consultative approach which involved regular face-to-face and telephone meetings with HR and Resourcing stakeholders to understand the challenges and to collaboratively develop the solution. As part of this, they worked with the client to understand what "good" looked like in the role, as well as whether there were any changes in requirements for the graduate role, compared to their understanding of the role from previous years. This allowed them to understand the qualities that would contribute to successful performance in the role, and a greater understanding of the improvement stakeholders wanted to see.

Weekly project calls were conducted to engage with the client and keep them up to date on key deliverables, risks and assumptions. A flexible approach to project management was applied throughout the project.

Outcome

Evaluation was built into the project plan, to evaluate the effectiveness of the solution against the four primary project objectives. This allowed the team to continue their evidence-based practice approach to the project through to the evaluation stage, by collecting large quantities of data from the four different sources of evidence (i.e. scientific literature, stakeholders, organisation and specialists/practitioners).

Evidence Collection

TMP supported the client's requirement to ensure a defensible, robust outcome. So, evidence- based evaluation approaches were outlined for the four project objectives.

- Objective 1: Positive Experience
  - Scientific literature used for comparison of video interview (VIV) Candidate Feedback to Candidate Feedback on other Assessment Methodology
  - Stakeholder impressions were collected via a Candidate Feedback Survey
- Objective 2: VIV as a Predictor of Performance
  - Scientific literature used for comparison of VIV method to alternative assessment methodology
  - Stakeholder feedback collected from Interviewers, on efficacy of VIV, and Assessor feedback was collected on candidate quality at Assessment Centre
  - At an organisational level, analysis was done to understand the spread of scores and conversion rates at Assessment Centre
  - Specialist input was collected via VIV benchmarking and quality checking exercise, as well as Lead Assessor and Senior Consultant experience feedback at Assessment Centre

- Objective 3: VIV to provide Fair Method
    - Scientific literature used for comparison of Adverse Impact (AI) results to best practice standards (such as AI of alternative assessment methods)
    - At an organisational level, analysis was done to understand AI data of VIV assessment stage, with comparison of VIV AI data to previous year's telephone interview (TIV) data
    - Specialist input was collected in VIV benchmarking and quality checking exercise
- Objective 4: VIV to offer efficiencies to the process
    - Scientific literature used review recruitment process data against anticipated efficiency benefits reported in the literature
    - Client feedback collected
    - At an organisational level, analysis was done to understand recruitment process data for 2019 in comparison to recruitment process data from 2018 (TIV process)

Particularly, concerning the third objective, "fair method," evaluation of the solution was extremely positive. Group differences in average scores for performance during the video interview stage were minimal. Candidates from minority and majority groups performed at a similar level, indicating reduced Adverse Impact and supporting a fair assessment process.

With the significant amount of investment that the NHS placed into the Graduate Management Training Scheme, this project formed an essential part of a wider initiative to simplify the selection process for trainees, maintain the quality of those trainees, and ultimately ensure that the pipeline of potential leaders within the NHS remained strong for the years ahead.

Acknowledgements

NHS Graduate Management Trainee Scheme

Kate Bradley

Susana Laranjeiro, University of the West of England

Psychology for Psychologists

Overview

Telephone interviews are a useful screening tool widely used in assessment, but they can be costly to organise and administer. Automated video interviews are an effective way to reduce administrative burden, but typically sacrifice the ability to tailor questions to individual candidates. Would it be possible to get the best of both options?

Saville Assessment partnered with Tazio to create a video interview powered by the Wave Professional Styles (Wave) behavioural assessment. Saville Assessment's Consultancy Team then used this tool in their own assessment process, to recruit Consultants. It enabled them to improve efficiency and increase the number, and quality, of candidates progressing through to the subsequent assessment stages.

Challenge

A few factors came together to inform this project, beyond the business need presented.

- As a provider of talent assessment solutions, it was imperative for Saville Assessment to get their selection processes right. After all, if they could not get it right for their own hires, how could they advise and support their clients?
- Their internal processes offered their Consultants an opportunity to pilot new products and innovations
- Transparency with their clients regarding their process allowed them to showcase their innovative portfolio developments; people they wanted to get excited about working with them

Setting Objectives

Their Consultancy Team took on the challenge of improving how they managed their Consultant vacancies, which typically attract 100 applicants per position. Consultants typically evaluated assessment solutions against a set of criteria. So, when starting this assessment campaign, they reviewed what they were looking to achieve in four areas.

- Quality: Assessments must identify the right people for the right roles
- Efficiency: Assessment performance should be gathered using as little organisational resource as possible. Completing assessments should take as little time as possible whilst assessing in a robust and fair way
- Engagement: Candidates should talk positively about their assessment experience
- Diversity and Inclusion: The diversity of a candidate pipeline should be upheld throughout each stage

In the campaign kick-off workshop, they agreed the focus had to be on two areas:

- Increasing the quality of candidates: Given the profile of Saville Assessment as an organisation they felt they could increase the number, and quality, of appointable candidates attending the assessment centre for their Consultant positions
- Making their process more efficient: The time the existing telephone interviews were taking to design and administer was identified as an issue. They wanted to deliver this campaign using less internal resource

They turned these considerations into SMART objectives. (SMART is an acronym for objectives which are Specific, Measurable, Attainable, Relevant and Time-based.) Specifically, in this campaign, they wanted to:

- Increase the number of candidates completing each stage of the process
- Increase the number of candidates attending the assessment centre who met the requirements for the role
- Reduce the administrative burden of organising, delivering, and assessing their existing telephone interviews

Approach

Historically, the company had used a three-stage assessment process:

- Stage 1: online assessments (behavioural and aptitude)
- Stage 2: telephone interview (with pre-set questions)
- Stage 3: assessment centre

The Consultants felt that Stages 1 and 3 were working well. However, they saw room for improvement in Stage 2, the telephone interview. They felt targeting this area of the assessment process would help achieve the specific objectives they had set themselves.

Practical Innovation

The Consultancy Team got together to consider ways to improve the telephone interview. They came up with the idea of aligning this stage of the assessment process with the approach they took to face-to-face interviews: a highly structured interview powered by a candidate's completion of the Wave questionnaire. The Wave questionnaire explores a person's motives, preferences, needs and talents within a work context. Research has demonstrated it to be a powerful predictor of a wide variety of performance and behaviour at work.

The Consultants felt that if they could create a video interview, where the interview questions were powered by a candidates' responses to the Wave questionnaire, they would meet their targets and have a new product which they had not come across in the market before. Candidates' experience would be improved by the personalisation of the interview experience, and the interview outputs would be enriched. The Consultants also recognised this product could benefit their clients with high volume recruitment processes. They therefore decided to replace the telephone interview with a video interview, powered by the Wave questionnaire assessment output.

The Consultants identified a partner to work with, for delivery of the video interview. They selected Tazio to provide candidates with an engaging experience. (See www.tazio.co.uk for details of this supplier's services.)

The New Process

In the new process, applicants to Saville Assessment's Consultant roles completed the Wave questionnaire and were assessed for their fit to the key behavioural requirements. As well as informing them whether they should be progressed to the next stage, it identified areas they would want to probe before committing resource to seeing them at the more expensive face-to-face stage.

If a candidate met the behavioural and aptitude requirements of the role, the integration they built with Tazio used the information from the assessments they had completed to present each candidate with a video interview bespoke to their responses. For example: if the candidate's responses to the Wave questionnaire suggested they have a challenge dealing with pressure, they would be asked, through the video interview, to reflect on a pressured situation they had encountered and share how they dealt with the difficulties that arose. The candidate's video interview responses enabled them to verify whether they were able to deal with the demands of the role.

Video interview questions were asked in relation to the four competencies they had identified as being most critical to the Consultant role. The outputs were then reviewed by Assessors at a time convenient to them with a clear audit trail stored in the Tazio interface.

Outcome

Notable Improvements

As there was no need to schedule the video interviews, with candidates completing them at a time convenient to them, the company saved significant administration time.

Following the success of this campaign, their integration with Tazio was updated, meaning candidates could be automatically progressed from online assessment to video interview with no time delay. This meant, from a candidate perspective, they could complete Stages 1 and 2 as one combined stage.

As the video interview questions were pulled from a bank of pre-designed questions dynamic to a candidate's responses, no additional design of video interview content was required. This was all automated based on their competency selection.

As the video interview questions were powered by Wave, they gained the benefits of the predictive validity associated with the Wave model.

By using an innovative approach to video assessment, the team showcased Saville Assessment to prospective recruits as an innovative, forward thinking organisation.

By auditing the scoring of their Assessors, they further ensured that they could have complete confidence in the consistency of scoring.

Results

The team achieved each of the objectives they set out in the kick-off meeting: increasing the number of candidates completing each stage of the process, increasing the number of candidates attending the assessment centre who met the requirements for the role, and reducing the administrative burden of organising, delivering, and assessing their existing telephone interviews.

There were also additional benefits from across the assessment effectiveness model:

- Quality: The number of candidates who completed Stage 2, were deemed to meet the requirements of the job description, and were therefore seen at assessment centre, increased from three in one hundred (from their previous campaign) to eight in one hundred
- Efficiency: They estimated a 75% reduction in administration requirement was achieved by:
  - removing the need to design a new telephone interview
  - removing the need for administration in scheduling interviews, including dealing with no-shows
  - managing Assessor resource in a more flexible way
- Engagement: There was a 25% increase in the number of candidates completing the video interview compared with the equivalent stage of the previous process
- Diversity and Inclusion: As the video interviews were completely standardised, the Consultants ensured there would be no additional opportunity for bias introduced by the interviewer as could be the case with a telephone interview

As a result of this case study, Saville Assessments have been able to show their clients how the solution works, and pilot the process for their high-volume recruiter clients.

Acknowledgements

Martin Kavanagh

Tom Stroud, CEO & Founder, Tazio

Tim Smith, Technical Director, Tazio

Maya Mistry, Consultant, Saville Assessment

Katie Thomas, Consultant Analyst, Saville Assessment

Section Two:
Beyond the Basics

In this section we share a selection of case studies which advance standard assessment practice in different ways. Some combine multiple approaches, introduce innovations in their development or delivery model, or show creativity in applying their findings.

In the first case study, EY's student recruitment team's approach to creating a level playing field for talented young people is explored.

Next, one of the UKs largest supermarkets' approach to recruitment, which applies the concepts of Fiero, Defamiliarisation and Flow, is explained.

Then, a look at assessment for individuals in high-stakes roles; specifically, Global Client Executives.

Fourth, Barclays shares their experience in creating an immersive recruitment process for their Graduate and Internship programmes, incorporating storytelling.

Followed by Allen & Overy, a leading international law firm, who created an engaging globally relevant approach to hiring the 'Lawyer of the Future.'

Penultimately, a well-established FMCG business' experience in creating a mid-level and future leader assessment process shows how they applied Business Psychology to identify candidates of the highest quality.

And in the final case study we learn, from a psychometric assessment provider, how they approached designing a truly international assessment tool.

The Inclusion Club

Overview

Commentators have often described Professional Service firms' leadership as, 'Pale, Male and Stale,' with female and BME incumbents finding it difficult to break into their leadership teams' 'Old Boys' Clubs.'

This topic has received a lot of attention in recent years and positive change can be seen. This case study shares the experience of one of the Big Four firms who showed courage to address this in a meaningful way.

As a major student recruiter, EY play an important role in helping to develop the UK's future business leaders and the skills of the UK workforce. They have taken bold steps to create a level playing field for talented young people looking to enter the profession, regardless of their background.

Challenge

As one of the UK's largest student recruiters, competing in an especially aggressive market, EY want to attract the best talent to grow their business. They believe that only the highest-performing teams, which maximise the power of different perspectives and voices, will succeed in the global marketplace.

EY recognised that there is unfortunately a strong link in the UK between socio-economic background, academic achievement and career prospects. Further, inequalities in professional firms are a function of inequalities in the country's education system. Top universities, for example, provide a springboard to the most coveted careers, yet access to them is often skewed towards the well-off, principally because these students generally perform better in exams. In addition, research has shown that students from lower socio-economic groups do not perform as well on certain ability tests, which can put them at a disadvantage.

Addressing these concerns raised significant challenges but the issues could not be ignored. In response, EY introduced a new student assessment and selection process that could be fairer and more inclusive, whilst maintaining the very highest intellectual standards.

Approach

A Strong Start

EY had previously introduced Strengths-based recruitment, moving away from the traditional competency-based assessments. Strengths-based assessment looks at past performance as evidence of capability but also uses future-focused techniques. Research (Seligman & Csikszentmihalyi, 2000, Linley & Kauffman, 2007, Harzer & Ruch, 2012, etc.) has shown that individuals who use their strengths at work are:

- more resilient
- happier
- have higher levels of self-esteem
- are more likely to stay in role
- perform at a higher level; and
- achieve their goals with less stress

Following the successful validation of the Strengths assessment process, EY conducted a detailed review of their recruitment process to see what else they could do.

Cause for Concern

An early-stage hurdle, which applied to most graduate recruitment programmes in the UK, was reference to UCAS points. The Universities and Colleges Admissions Service in the UK (UCAS) uses points to measure the relative value of all post-16 qualifications in the UK, with points assigning a numerical score to the possible grades that can be achieved in each type of qualification. Selection based on these criteria was becoming increasingly incongruent with the social mobility agenda, and links between career success and UCAS points remained unclear (Kirkup, et al., 2008).

EY's review considered the impact of the academic screening criteria they had set at the time, i.e. 300 UCAS points, and 2:1 degree. They recognised that:

- There was a lack of evidence that academic performance was predictive of subsequent on-the-job performance

- Inclusive progress would be hampered by applying strict academic criteria, as there was a strong link between socio-economic background, academic achievement, and future career prospects
- Academic screening had inherent anomalies and inconsistencies; for example, a candidate with a 2.2 in Mechanical Engineering from a highly academic university may be excluded from applying whilst a candidate with 2.1 from a less demanding degree programme at a less academic University could be eligible
- Experienced professional hires, joining EY later in their careers, could have successful careers even though they would not have been eligible to join the student programmes due to academic screening requirements

Change for the Better

As a result, EY made three bold changes to their recruitment process.

- EY removed their academic 300 UCAS points, and 2:1 degree screening criteria
- They stopped asking candidates about their prior work experience or positions of responsibility held on their application form
- They began operating a 'CV blind' recruitment process so Interviewers and Assessors would not have access to a candidate's application form as part of the recruitment process

In order to do this, a re-design of the process was required to ensure it was robust enough to identify the best and most appropriate talent for the business whilst maintaining a level playing field for candidates to be assessed.

The New Process

The process was underpinned by the Strengths-based recruitment methodology. This approach helped support students with less access to work experience and careers guidance by focusing on potential rather than experience.

A multi-assessment approach was also adopted which combined a range of tests (strengths, technology mindset, numerical and verbal reasoning) that candidates completed in one go rather than in separate assessments. The test scores were then combined into one single talent score, meaning a fairer method of scoring, enabling candidates to demonstrate their capability across a broader set of criteria.

The new assessment process incorporated significant changes:

- Candidates were no longer required to have a minimum academic requirement to make an application
- Candidates were no longer required to submit a CV or covering letter as part of their application; they provided their contact details and completed an 'equal opportunities' form
- Prior work experience and/or positions of responsibility no longer formed part of the screening criteria
- All candidates were given coaching prior to their first interview to provide all students with an equal opportunity to succeed
- A 'CV blind' interview process; details of a candidate's application were only visible to the EY Student Recruitment team, not the Interviewers

This created an assessment process that EY felt was free from discrimination, allowing candidates to perform to the best of their ability, creating opportunities for many students who in previous years may have been rejected due to arbitrary screening criteria.

Outcome

EY continue to value students' academic achievements and maintain high intellectual standards. However, they feel that changes to the process levelled the playing field, allowing all candidates the chance to apply, and significantly supported their commitment to Diversity and inclusiveness addressing the social mobility challenge.

Moving to an upfront multi-assessment approach enabled the business to consider an additional c.15,000 candidates at the initial screening stage, rather than rejecting candidates in a sequential, singular model.

When analysing their intake in the following year, they found the diversity improved:

- 45% female
- 30% black and minority ethnic (BME)
- 60% state school educated
- 37% first generation to go to university
- 9% eligible for free school meals

Upon further analysis it was revealed that 18.3% of graduates who joined the firm, and 18.5% of school leavers, would have previously been ineligible to apply due to minimum grade requirements. In addition to the above hiring statistics, the below key milestones were achieved:

– No Adverse Impact was identified throughout the process for any demographic group

– All assessment stages positively correlated, thus predicting success at later stages of the process

– Process efficiencies reduced time-to-offer by 35%

– Process improvements reduced the demand on Assessors and Interviewers, returning 4,000 client hours to the business

Acknowledgements

Capp & Co Ltd

EY Graduate Talent teams

Fiero, Defamiliarisation and Flow

Overview

The retail sector is one of the UK's largest employers, it is fast-paced and has unique challenges. Consumer needs constantly evolve. Retail failures get a lot of negative attention (e.g. nationwide store closures by Toys R Us, Maplin and BHS). Roles in this sector can be difficult to fill. And, according to the Institute of Student Employers (ISE) Development Survey, it has amongst the highest attrition rates of any sector for graduate roles.

In this context, one of the UKs largest supermarkets decided to partner with Business Psychologists to address their challenges in recruiting future leaders. Morrisons, working with talent consultancy Amberjack, created a novel recruitment process for authentic assessment, applying concepts of Fiero, Defamiliarisation and Flow.

Challenge

WM Morrison Supermarkets PLC (trading as 'Morrisons'), serves millions of customers each week from hundreds of stores, as one of the largest supermarkets in the UK. They retained Business Psychologists to work with them to improve their future leader recruitment process, in a competitive graduate recruitment market with tech-savvy candidates.

Unlike their competitors, Morrisons do not just sell food, they make it. As one of the UK's biggest food producers, recruitment needed to reflect their "field to fork" operation and provide a realistic and authentic preview of what it's like to work at Morrisons. Crucial aspects of Morrisons culture (resilience, self-awareness, learning agility) also needed to be measured for better candidate fit, to impact attrition rates. Morrisons needed a market-leading, exciting and innovative process that would better position their unique proposition.

The company also needed to ensure internal stakeholders trusted the process. Related to which, they needed to assess candidates' potential to be successful, rather than experience alone, given their age profile.

Morrisons partnered with Amberjack with the objective of increasing the right candidates' interest in Morrisons, and better predicting which candidates would be successful in their roles. And all of this had to be underpinned by principles of Business Psychology, rigour and best practice.

In considering the approach to be taken, evidence from a number of sources was considered including:

- Amberjack's "Future Talent Insights" research; analysis of predictive effectiveness of selection tools in relation to assessment criteria
- Amberjack's high potential (HiPo) Framework
- Amberjack's experience
- Morrisons' business insight: stakeholder's interviews extracting issues and objectives
- Academic research, which highlighted important characteristics for effective behavioural assessment solutions:
  - consistent and clear
  - job relevance
  - providing candidates opportunity to show what they know
  - treating candidates with respect

The Practitioners cited reference to: Hausknecht, et al., 2004, Truxillo, Bodner, Bertolino, Bauer & Yonce, 2009, Anderson, Salgado & Hülsheger, 2010.

Approach

Stakeholder management and buy-in was crucial for the Practitioners to elicit the business insight needed for transformation. Success was to be measured through reduced attrition, fill rates, conversions and stakeholder face validity.

Solution Design

Workshops and Job Analysis (at the Visionary, Subject Matter Expert (SME) and Incumbent levels) were critical to build up a bank of realistic job simulations, as well as develop a detailed behaviourally anchored assessment framework fundamentally reflective of Morrisons' Ways of Working.

A bespoke process and assessment exercises were designed incorporating the following principles:

- Fiero: a neuroscientific concept, Fiero drives engagement and loyalty and is triggered by stretching challenges that allows one to showcase capability
- Flow: as defined by Mihaly Csikszentmihalyi, a state within which one can assess innate strengths, reducing contamination from socially desirable or learned behaviours
- Defamiliarisation: a tool for creating a sense of 'Flow,' defamiliarisation exercises put candidates in unfamiliar situations without clear rules allowing an authentic assessment of resilience and agility
- Assessment of 'High Potential,' using Amberjack's High Potential Framework which has as core principles:
  - Learning Agility
  - Self-Awareness
  - Resilience
  - Motivational Drive
- Reflection: both through reflective interviews and through a decompression session after the defamiliarisation exercise, allowing the Practitioners to assess candidates' self-awareness and discuss relative strengths when in a disarmed state
- Immersion and Realistic Job Preview (RJP): attrition on the Morrisons Future Leader programmes seemed to be largely driven by candidates not understanding the roles applied for. It was therefore critical that all assessments were reflective of reality
- Face Validity: essential to building internal trust, as candidates performing well in previous assessments often had not been offered employment because stakeholders had not seen their capabilities demonstrated in a context they felt was valid

While the assessment framework formed the basis of all assessment processes, the content was tailored to reflect the reality of the different roles available. The end-to-end solution was delivered on Amberjack's immersive, interactive and video-driven technology platforms.

The Recruitment Process

The process started with an SJT offering an initial RJP. It then moved to a video interview that consisted of future-focused scenario-based questions, which brought to life the reality of the schemes' demands (e.g. nightshifts in cold warehouses, not knowing what your next rotation will be, etc.).

The culmination was the Assessment Centres, which were held at function specific locations: for example, manufacturing plants. The Practitioners developed bespoke materials for each function and delivered a true day-in-the-life experience using exercises reflective of the realities of the job.

The Logistics and Manufacturing defamiliarisation exercise was arguably the single most transformative assessment designed. Candidates had no information about what was going to happen, and the exercise was not part of the event schedule. They were asked to deliver a briefing to warehouse colleagues using fragments of information about a situation where machinery was 'breaking down,' impacting deliveries. This exercise was delivered in a real warehouse setting with real Morrisons employees heckling and playing the part of disgruntled colleagues. It lasted eight minutes. It tested resilience, an essential element of the High Potential framework, in an unexpected, authentic and realistic way. Candidates relied on their natural behaviour, in 'flow,' to manage the unscripted situation. They also needed to demonstrate their agility, another key element of the High Potential framework, by responding rapidly to new information and circumstances, as well as coping with ambiguity and incomplete information. Regardless of how they performed, candidates emerged energised as a result of having been in a state of 'Flow' and from the Fiero that comes from overcoming such an unexpected challenge. Afterwards, the decompression session allowed them to reflect on how they performed. Assessors were therefore able to evaluate self-awareness and motivational drive, the other essential elements of the Amberjack High Potential framework.

Stakeholders were involved in co-development of all processes, tools and exercises. The Practitioners believe that all stakeholders bought into the approach because it was inclusive. Regular feedback, detailed planning and milestones provided clarity at all times.

Outcome

Delivery Process

The company's recruitment became more about self-selection from beginning to end. The mobile and immersive process was automated, incorporating strong elements of interactivity, problem solving, tests of skill and challenges specific to Morrisons. Candidates were assessed against ways of working, behaviours and roles using Amberjack's

HiPo framework and pioneering approach to interviewing; future-focused scenario-based questions. This delivered more emphasis on role-fit and future potential, rather than past-experience, and its effectiveness was evident by the improvement in attrition.

In total, 3,600 hours were spent on planning, system set up and implementation of this solution. It was scalable which meant that it was up and running within a matter of weeks.

Learning derived specifically applied to co-designing the solution with Morrisons stakeholders. The Practitioners reported that the feedback was overwhelming from the recruitment team, senior business leaders, future leaders on the programmes, and others. They recognised that a process was needed to capture information so that it could be used effectively. This issue was identified quickly and addressed, so it did not cause any delays and resulted in more efficient analysis.

In total Morrisons made 112 hires from over 10,800 applications across 12 different programmes. The new recruitment process was designed to be consumer-centric and to meet the aspirational needs of young future leaders. The results achieved were expressed in qualitative and quantitative ways.

Candidate Feedback

"Overall, it's been an excellent process. There have been a wide variety of tasks and the process has been easy to follow. My favourite activity was the unexpected activity at the Assessment Centre [Defamiliarisation Exercise]. It was modern and innovative, not something I've ever done before. The unexpected exercise was challenging and made you think on your feet but also very interesting to be put in a possible real-life situation." - *Julien Vetterhoeffer, Logistics Graduate Scheme*

"I've found the recruitment process very well organised. Everyone I've spoken to has been approachable and friendly, helping me as much as they can. The most enjoyable part for me was the unexpected exercise during the Assessment Centre, it brought to life real situations that could happen in a day to day role at Morrisons." - *Ben Barker, Graduate Scheme*

Return on Investment

In total 1,800 candidates attended the 60 Assessment Centres, with conversion rates increasing to 43% from 30%. Holding Assessment Centres at function specific locations also seemed to improve authenticity. The level of confidence in recruitment as expressed by stakeholders means the transformation made by the Practitioners and inclusive process built by them was the sole driver in contributing to the outstanding success achieved.

The new process reportedly delivered a 10% reduction in like-for-like costs year-on-year, and graduate roles were filled eight months earlier. Attrition was lowered to under 5% against 17% from the previous cohort, compared to the industry average of 10.4% and a sector average of 18% (ISE Development Survey 2017). Candidates also claimed to find the new process fast; on average 17% quicker than industry benchmarks.

Stakeholder Feedback

"At Morrisons we like to be innovative, and our new Future Leaders Assessment process is truly innovative from beginning to end. If I had to name my favourite element of the process it must be the unexpected activity at the Assessment Centre, just the reaction of the candidates and involving some of our own people, our team managers and our colleagues from the shop floor, role playing along with the candidates has been fantastic. We can really trust the assessments we make, and candidates really know what they're signing up for!" - *Adele Holtom, People Specialist – Training Wakefield Logistics Scheme Lead.*

Acknowledgements

Sophie Meaney, Managing Director, Consulting Solutions & Strategic Development, Amberjack

Fran Cousans, Principal Consultant, Amberjack

Sebastien Kenneally Miles, Assessment Consultant, Amberjack

Jessica Kipling, Assessment Consultant, Amberjack

Ali Guest, Senior People Manager, Talent, WM Morrison Supermarkets PLC

Emma Cooksley, People Manager, Early Careers, WM Morrisons Supermarkets PLC

Client Executive Assessment

Overview

Atos is a European multinational information technology service and consulting company with offices worldwide. It specialises in hi-tech transactional services, unified communications, cloud, big data and cybersecurity. The success of Atos' largest client engagements is the responsibility of the Global Client Executive (CEX) assigned to the account.

As the organisation transforms to address the challenges and opportunities of their industry, the demands on their CEX population evolve. They called on Business Psychologists to help them get a clearer view of the capabilities of their CEXs around the world, and to prepare them to make an even greater contribution in future.

Challenge

Atos was built over many years, through a series of mergers and acquisitions. As a result, their Global CEX population had different backgrounds, with different levels of capability and experience. Further, Atos had a presence in over 70 countries, with significant cultural diversity, and an "inconsistent approach to talent management." They defined a global strategic plan to move away from a traditional technology-driven sales approach to a more consultative holistic solution. So, when they undertook a transformation of their operating model, they decided to also review the capabilities they required of CEX role holders.

The Consultants at Business Psychology consultancy, Zircon, recognised the challenges facing Atos were not exceptional for an organisation operating in a 'VUCA world.' VUCA is an acronym first used in 1987, drawing on the leadership theories of Warren Bennis and Burt Nanus, to describe the volatility, uncertainty, complexity and ambiguity of conditions and situations. Originally referenced in military settings, it has been used increasingly in reference to the business world since the turn of the century. The challenges it describes bring focus to organisational leadership demands, for foresight and insight, to adapt and capture opportunities in a world where change is unpredictable (Sullivan, 2012, Kinsinger & Walch, 2012, Caron, 2009).

Within this world, the Business Psychologists felt that it was imperative that Atos be enabled to develop their employees to have a diverse skill set. Understanding the macro-challenges and the impact on talent was therefore key to success.

They needed to identify which CEX 'got it' and were high performing in the context of the macro, global, digital environment; significantly and consistently outperforming their peers. They wanted to identify the top 10% of Atos global talent.

Zircon supported Atos to:

- Identify macro-challenges facing Atos (globalisation, digitalisation, pace of change, legislation, economy, and competition)
- Define the requirements of Atos CEX in the external, digital context
- Assess the capability of Atos to meet the external market requirements and conduct data driven assessment for development
- Broaden the understanding of the talent across the Atos sales population through a virtual, digital solution
- Encourage individuals to develop and champion their own career path
- Integrate a standard level of assessment across the CEX employee lifecycle
- Create clear criteria for success to encourage a common language
- Challenge the business to understand the gaps between the macro-challenges and the capability and fit of the global population
- Re-define the people, talent strategy, and plan given the core strengths and gaps for the future

Approach

Research

The team needed to research and define what "great" looked like for the CEX role of the future. This was done via critical stakeholder interviews, with high-potential employees and senior stakeholders globally, as well as an online card sort exercise to identify the micro and macro factors impacting digital transformation and success.

The critical talent requirements needed for Atos to address their challenges were identified using BeTalent's model of potential. Following seven years' research, BeTalent produced the BEST+ model, made up of Behaviours, Expertise, Strengths (McKinsey, 2011) Tenets (MacRae & Furnham, 2014), Aspirations, Engagement, Emotional, Social and Learning Agility/Cognitive Intelligence. These dimensions combine to form the potential model. From this model, the team identified the critical requirements for high performance in the CEX role.

Design

The Consultants designed a data driven virtual assessment event for a development programme. It offered a remote assessment solution for the global population, thus saving travel time, cost and pollution. It included:

- An online pre-assessment tool, including the BeTalent Decision Styles and Strengths Insight, and a tailored 360° feedback tool, allowing the individual to see themselves from different perspectives
- A two-hour face-to-face Skype (video call) assessment, which examined aspirations, values and fit with requirements
- A personal feedback session for each CEX, with a behavioural Psychologist, and personalised development discussion to explore their strengths and development areas

This enabled Atos to identify talent, as well as offering the employees an insight on their strengths, empowering them for future success.

Process

The role of the assessment team was to challenge the CEXs about their operating style, given the macro-challenges, and to help them to create a personal plan.

All data was collated and analysed to understand the themes, gaps and risks for the business.

The conclusions were used to inform talent strategy and focus for the company's immediate future.

As well as remaining in regular contact with the project team at Atos, the Business Psychologists were actively encouraging Atos to change their views on talent. The global data was critical when influencing Atos to think about talent differently and understand related risks. As a result, Atos re-wrote their talent strategy to reflect the global digitalisation and transformation of the world in which they operate.

Outcome

The Atos Global Head of Human Resources (HR), Sales & Markets, expressed overwhelming approval with the project, stating: "As a result of the programme, we are clear on our expectations of a CEX. The CEX Blueprint, with the resultant 11 talent requirements, universally informs our approach to talent management. Our CEXs are clear on what is expected, their relative level of competence today, and the key areas of focus to improve their performance. All CEXs have benefitted from additional one-to-one coaching from Zircon, in order to digest their feedback. One hundred percent of our CEXs have an agreed Individual Development Plan."

"We are aware of the collective strengths/areas of development and have built this into our supporting CEX Leadership Development Programme. Areas of priority including Emotional and Social Intelligence had not been previously addressed."

"Some employees have concluded that the new CEX role is not for them. In a supportive environment, many are finding or have secured alternative roles in Atos. These employees are being replaced by internal and external talents, who are required to undertake the Strengths Insight and EI Questionnaires in order to ensure a robust appointment process, whilst simultaneously identifying development needs."

When asked to respond to the statement, "I believe the assessment for development programme will help me with my career development," respondents were largely positive:

- 27% selected 'Excellent'
- 40% selected 'Very Good'
- 24% selected 'Good'
- 4% selected 'OK,' none selected 'Below Expectations,' and 5% did not respond

Acknowledgements

Dr Amanda Potter BSc (Hons) MSc AfBPSs HMABP CPsychol CSci

Helen Hargrave

Story-Based Assessment

Overview

Barclays 'helps people achieve their ambitions, in the right way.' This purpose was central to the development of a new immersive recruitment process for their Graduate and Internship programmes.

The Bank's ambition was to provide a unique and educational experience for candidates, enabling them to learn more about the banking sector, the programmes and themselves. This was achieved using a novel approach which combined ability, technical competence, and cultural fit assessments in a real-life, interactive case study.

Challenge

Barclays wanted to create an efficient recruitment process, using the latest recruitment technology, combining authentic content and relevant motivational, cognitive and technical assessments. They intended for the process to be efficient, enabling both the candidates and the business to make informed decisions on individuals' alignment to a programme, whilst improving the candidate experience.

Opportunities for Improvement

As a starting point, Barclays identified issues with their recruitment process that the new solution needed to address.

The process needed to be fully aligned to specific business areas. Barclays wanted to ensure that the experience they provided allowed candidates to gain a better understanding of not only Banking and Barclays but also the individual programmes. Therefore, the process was to be designed to reveal more in-depth and tailored content as the candidate advanced through the multiple stages. This would mean candidates and the business would be required to invest more effort and time towards the end of the process, than up-front.

The move towards a fully automated process in the early stages of application provided a more time-efficient solution. Candidates should complete the initial stages of the process with no requirement for Assessor intervention, managing it in their own time, improving their overall experience.

Barclays also wanted to gain a better understanding of each candidate through the collection of relevant data. By introducing advanced technology at the start of their process, Barclays could ensure only the most appropriate candidates progressed, on the basis of fair criteria. With diversity as a priority, automated collection of detailed data on candidates would give Barclays the confidence to remove arbitrary screening criteria, giving access to the programmes to a much broader range of students. (For example, they needed to remove potential barriers in the early stage, such as academic achievement or CV requirements.) In addition, the use of technology (rather than Assessors) would help remove unconscious bias in the first stages – focusing on candidates' true potential and motivation for Barclays and their programme.

Specific Objectives

To ensure the innovation met the brief, the project stakeholders set clear, measurable objectives:

- Create Best in Class Candidate Experience:
  - Create a recruitment experience that would immerse candidates into the Barclays culture, provide an in-depth understanding of the candidates' chosen programme and excite them about the potential future with the bank
  - Deliver this experience through the latest recruitment technology to enable a unique, seamless and interactive experience which candidates could complete in their own time
  - Provide relevant feedback to candidates regardless of what stage they reached
  - Build knowledge of the sector and programme through authentic content

- Support Business Performance:
  - Design a process which positions Barclays as a forward-thinking and innovative organisation
  - Implement technology and tools that allow for a fair process using more data points, learning more about candidates up-front, allowing better understanding and consistent decisions
  - Improve efficiency of the process and reduce business time and resource
  - Revalidate assessment criteria to ensure it is fit for purpose, develop a complete understanding of what determines graduate success and support their future development upon joining the business

Approach

By placing the candidate at the heart of the solution, Barclays created a recruitment experience that was genuinely innovative on a number of levels.

Tools Designed

The new assessment platform delivered a fully immersive, multi-stage process with interactive and engaging content at each stage.

- Business Insights 1: Candidates were presented a short series of four documentary style dramas that represent real life dilemmas that face banking; this was the candidate's first introduction to the bank. There were break points in the drama when candidates answered questions relating to their strengths and cognitive abilities (multi-assessment approach). This interactive stage led to the removal of standard psychometric tests and enabled candidates to demonstrate their broader ability, giving Barclays a 'whole' person view of the potential graduate

- Business Insights 2: The narrative continued. Candidates would complete a business line specific in-tray exercise that reflected a real piece of analysis graduates carried out in these roles. This included manager introductions and pre-recorded questions, and asked graduates to respond using the latest video interview technology. This technology ensured all candidates had a consistent experience and removed potential Interviewer/Assessor bias

- Business Interview: Managers would conduct live video or telephone interviews. Interviews included motivational, technical, strengths and values-based questions marked against a consistent framework

- Barclays Business Meeting: The narrative continued and concluded. Barclays managers observed candidates responding to an immersive challenge. The exercises were specific to the graduate programme the candidate had applied for. Candidates were asked to pre-prepare some information prior to attending to ensure that candidates who did not have prior experience or knowledge of banking had a level playing field to compete on

Each candidate was provided with an automated, customised feedback report which focused on highlighting their top three strengths, and how they could develop these further for future success. They were also offered the opportunity to have a career coaching call with a Barclays employee.

Increased Inclusion

Barclays were the first Bank in the UK to fully remove CV and academic criteria as part of the screening process, which eliminated a number of the initial barriers. This was a step forward both in terms of improving the candidate experience and creating a fully inclusive process. This was made possible by implementing a solution driven by data and underpinned by the strengths methodology, which focused on candidate potential and motivation rather than past experience.

The immersive, story-telling approach created a common thread that ran throughout the process, not only allowing candidates to demonstrate their capability but also making the experience engaging and fun. The first stages of the process leveraged the latest recruitment technologies combining multiple assessment into one video-based, interactive experience, putting the candidate in charge.

The authentic content used to create the solution not only educated the candidates about the sector, but also meant that Barclays could have tailored assessments for individual programmes, of which there were nine in total.

Project Management

The project, to create this process, was to be delivered in an exceptionally short period of time (about four months). Meeting project deadlines necessitated active engagement from all stakeholders, addressed by setting up a strategic working group. In addition, Barclays worked closely with their assessment partner, Capp & Co, to create clear project plans and deliverables and to ensure project milestones did not slip.

Outcome

Create Best in Class Candidate Experience

Utilisation of recruitment technology had significantly reduced the amount of time candidates were required to invest upfront and gave flexibility to the candidates to complete the assessment in their own time and environment.

Every candidate, regardless of which stage they reached in the process, was provided with a personalised feedback report providing information on their top three strengths and how to develop them further.

Candidate Feedback

Barclays asked candidates to respond to the following question in an anonymous feedback form, "What have you learnt from the assessment process that makes you look forward to working for Barclays?" From the initial review, there were six key themes in terms of response:

- Barclays is innovative
- Barclays is fast paced and exciting
- You will get the opportunity to grow and develop at Barclays
- The assessment gives a real insight to what you will actually do at Barclays
- It is engaging and challenging
- It is different to anything candidates have done previously

Candidates free-text responses included:

- "This is new, this is different, it's likely to stand out and I think you're really testing us in the ways in which we need for this role"
- "I've learnt from the assessment process about the real-life situations which I may face in the role which have obviously forced me to use my brain and have pushed me to think that this is something that I really look for in a career"
- "I really want to join Barclays because I like people that make original things, that have new ideas, and that use technology, it's what you're doing even with the process of recruiting, so this originality really appeals to me"

Supporting Business Performance

The new framework was implemented across the business, leading to consistency in approach despite what programme candidates apply to.

The strengths-based approach allowed Barclays to focus on creating an assessment solution that was based on future potential, rather than past experiences.

Inclusion

This methodology, combined with the multi-assessment approach, provided a more in-depth analysis of candidates. This allowed Barclays to remove initial barriers to application including academic criteria and CV upload both of which were known up-front barriers to application.

There was no Adverse Impact occurring against gender, ethnicity or age overall within any business area. In its first year, hiring metrics collected showed:

- 26,401 applications from over 1,700 universities
- 31% applications from female candidates, 47% BAME and 4% LGBT
- 36% increase in applications from candidates from disadvantaged backgrounds
- 266 offers from 106 universities
- 31% female hires, 43% BAME and 4% LGBT

Acknowledgements

Barclays

Capp & Co

Selecting for the Future

Overview

Allen & Overy (A&O) is a leading international law firm comprising over 5,500 people in 44 offices across 31 countries. Like all law firms, they are confronted with the realities of how the practice of law is changing. For example, lawyers no longer have a monopoly on the field. From legal document technicians to virtual law offices and self-help legal websites, today's lawyers face competition from a variety of non-lawyer sources. Technology has also transformed the practice of law and lawyers must become proficient in a wide range of technology platforms. Outsourcing of legal work to foreign countries is another challenging economic reality.

Recruiters at A&O responded pragmatically with their 'Lawyer of the Future' project which defined the skills and qualities the firm were looking for in their future lawyers. They then partnered with Amberjack to define recruitment practices that would enable A&O to attract and recruit these 'future lawyers' globally.

Challenge

With a generation of candidates submerged within a technology driven landscape, innovation lay the heart of their needs. For A&O, it was essential to provide 'lawyer of the future' candidates with a realistic job preview, showcasing the challenges a trainee lawyer would face at A&O, whilst providing an outstanding candidate experience.

A&O wanted the new selection process to be immersive and engaging yet challenging, to drive loyalty and provide a realistic job preview. Translating the automation and efficiencies that A&O had within their firm into the candidate experience was therefore important.

With an ever-growing candidate pool, it was fundamental to ensure that candidates had a positive experience, regardless of the outcome. Automation of the process was essential to effectively deal with recruitment volume. They chose to work with Business Psychologists at Amberjack to ensure a robust refresh for their Early Careers recruitment, for Training Contract hires.

Approach

Amberjack's solution included changes to both the sifting and selection stages of the process. This involved not only re-designing interviews but, most significantly, the introduction of an immersive video based Situational Judgement Test (SJT) to sift out candidates at the start of the process. The SJT was made up of job-related scenarios, designed to assess how a candidate would respond to typical scenarios they might face in the role.

Applying Science

Evidence for the approach came from:

- Amberjack's "Future Talent Insights" research; analysis of predictive effectiveness of selection tools in relation to assessment criteria
- Candidate experience considerations, with 60% of companies saying that candidate experience was very important (the highest rank of a 1-10 scale) in a 2018 report
- Considering diversity and social mobility, as SJTs have less Adverse Impact towards minority groups (Lievens, Peeters & Shollaert, 2008) and have high favourability ratings from candidates (Lievens, 2013)
- Using a realistic job preview, as these have been shown to be important in the recruitment process (Breaugh, 2017), feeding into candidate expectations as well as job satisfaction once in the role (Bilal & Bashir, 2016)
- Referencing academic research around storytelling to engage the listener authentically and help them to understand the situation in a more meaningful way (Suzuki, et al., 2018)

Solution Design

To ensure A&O were assessing candidates on the basis of attributes defined for the 'Lawyer of the Future,' a total of 55 Partners, Senior Associates/Associates and Trainees were interviewed by Amberjack Assessment Consultants. The interviews explored their roles, values and 'what good might look like' in the future at A&O. Thematic analysis was used on this rich data, along with mapping to the existing 'Lawyer of the Future' framework and Amberjack's High Potential assessment framework. This enabled the Designers to differentiate the 'acceptable' from the 'exceptional.' In addition to gaining this insight, the job analyses were critical to building a bank of realistic job scenarios for the SJT and interview questions.

Using the bank of realistic scenarios obtained from the job analyses, situations that provided a real-life preview of the job were created. Following this, subject matter expert trials validated the items in terms of culture and authenticity, enabling the final set of scenarios to be chosen and creatively linked together to tell the story of life at A&O. The output was an SJT like no other, showcasing different locations and projects within a 24-hour period. Given the global scale of the business, they were inspired by the theme 'the sun never sets', demonstrating that there is always someone doing something extraordinary at work.

Central to the design of the SJT was the use of storytelling. Through storytelling, certain reactions in the brain take place, making the content even more compelling. Via neural coupling, listeners connect the story to their own ideas and experiences (speaker–listener neural coupling underlies successful communication per Stephens, Silbert & Hasson, 2010). At the same time, dopamine is released into the system making it easier to remember more accurately. (Denenberg, Kima & Palmiter, 2003). Finally, activity in the cortex takes place, making fact processing much easier. Together, these activities lead to a more meaningful, memorable and moving experience. Storytelling for the SJT was anchored in the job analysis findings and more specifically, the A&O themes: supportive, international, friendly, high performing and innovative.

The SJT was filmed from a third-person perspective whereby the candidate follows four characters around A&O office locations in New York, London, Frankfurt and Singapore. The disparate scenarios were connected using geographical captions and timestamps, orientating the candidate through the 24 hours. Interactions between the characters in the scenarios include in-person and video conference conversations to demonstrate the global scale of the business and the breadth of opportunities. A final addition to the SJT was a ticking clock, demonstrating time moving throughout the 24-hour period, but also bringing an element of pace and dynamism.

The second stage of the solution involved designing an interview question bank for the final stage interview. It combined A&O's competency-based style questions and new future-focused scenario-based questions (FFSBQs) to help assess future potential. The

Designers ensured these questions promoted social mobility and inclusion. FFSBQs are designed not to reward past performance over future potential; because whether or not a person had an opportunity to do something in the past would not be an accurate indicator of whether they would have the capability to do it in future.

Outcome

As a result of this project an immersive and engaging, yet challenging, recruitment process was deployed. It increased recruiter confidence in the hiring decisions being made, strengthened the A&O brand, and provided a superior candidate experience. It also increased objectivity, in terms of looking for future potential and not relying on school type or attainment to appraise candidates.

Over five months 1,117 hours were spent on the planning, design, system set up and implementation of the SJT, with the process going live in time for the 2019 Graduate intake. The high-quality, innovative SJT platform design exceeded both the client and candidates' expectations whilst also efficiently deselecting unsuitable candidates.

Adverse impact analysis was carried out on the SJT after the first 152 completions. The Psychologists measured whether applying a certain benchmark systematically negatively affected selection rates for the protected characteristics of gender, ethnicity and disability. A benchmark was set where there was no Adverse Impact against these protected groups with a 30% sift of candidates at this stage.

Other outcomes as a result of the improved process included:

- Over 3,700 candidates completing the SJT in the months following deployment
- A reasonable adjustment, text-based version of the SJT also went live, leading to an inclusive, technology enabled process

A large-scale predictive validity and Adverse Impact analysis of the assessment tools was later carried out, in partnership with Amberjack, to substantiate the success of the selection process.

Acknowledgements

Sophie Meaney, Managing Director, Consulting Solutions & Strategic Development, Amberjack

Jessica Kipling, Assessment Consultant, Amberjack

Debbie Kirwan, Consulting Solutions Director, Amberjack

Gareth Dimelow, Creative Director, Amberjack

Hannah Rolph, Graduate Recruitment Manger, Allen & Overy LLP

Danielle Trawick, Senior Manager, Global Recruiting & Employer Brand, Allen & Overy LLP

Tarek Dawas, Global Head of Resourcing, Allen & Overy LLP

Lee Hollands, Director, OCD Media Ltd

Paul Dodd, Director, OCD Media Ltd

Different by Design

Overview

A well-established FMCG business, with over a century of successful operations, attributed much of their success to their great people, in great teams within their great place to work. So, attracting talent was not hard. But ensuring their selection process delivered the best candidates, who would support their brand differentiation in their market, was essential.

They decided to implement a direct recruitment model for mid-level and future leaders, a population that was critical to sustaining their culture and their continued success. This enabled them to take ownership of their candidate value proposition, create a fantastic candidate experience, and identify and recruit candidates of the highest quality.

Noteworthy in this case example is the level of commitment shown by the client organisation to doing things properly. Read on to find out how they applied best practice Business Psychology along the way.

Challenge

Effectively selecting external talent is fundamental to any organisation's success, especially in highly competitive markets with constantly changing demands.

Adding to that complexity for this organisation was their global spread; they had operations in over 150 countries, managing over 200 brands. They needed to capitalise on the efficiencies that could be achieved with uniform solutions, without overlooking the distinctive needs of their many markets.

Having previously worked with a Business Psychology Consultancy to develop their Leadership Capability framework, they wanted this embedded too.

They invited Business Psychologists to help them identify assessment solutions for implementation that would be applicable to all leadership roles, across all functions, in all regions, aligned to their brand, offering an experience appropriate to an 'Employer of Choice,' so that even unsuccessful candidates could have a positive experience.

The Business Psychologists recognised that customised assessment tools would be required; and that extensive training would be required to ensure the successful deployment of the solution.

Approach

Solution Selection

The Psychologists proposed using online assessment tools for an initial sift, to identify suitable applicants early in the process based on relevant drivers of performance. This offered a low cost, low effort, reliable solution. But diverse and customised tools needed to be used to meet the broad brief. They selected:

- A culture match assessment, as alignment between personal values and organisational values typically correlates with employee engagement (Boury, et al., 2013)
- Cognitive ability tests, as cognitive ability has been demonstrated to predict performance better than ability, trait, disposition or job experience measures (Schmitt & Hunter, 2004)
- A bespoke leadership preference questionnaire, as Big Five personality models have been shown to consistently correlate with job performance (Barrick & Mount, 1991)

Additionally, for candidates successful at the initial sift stage, face-to-face Assessment Centre exercises were proposed, as Schmitt & Hunter, 1998, showed that Assessment Centre exercises can be one of the best predictors of job performance.

Research

Extensive research was undertaken to collect a broad perspective on the demands of the roles, around the world.

- Job analysis was conducted to gather a representative sample of views about what made an excellent leader in the client's environment
- Multiple focus groups were conducted in each of the four regions operated in: Europe, the Americas, Asia and Africa
  - Participants included relevant stakeholders and job incumbents
  - The focus groups covered what was needed to be a leader in knowledge, skills, abilities (KSAs), culture and personality

- Interviews were conducted with 19 senior talent subject matter experts, again revolving around what was required of an excellent leader in each category
- Additionally, two questionnaires were circulated:
  - In the job analysis questionnaire, 291 job incumbents globally were asked to specify the critically important KSAs and personality traits of a leader in the organisation, as well as how they should handle a positive and negative critical incident
  - A culture analysis questionnaire was administered to 39 subject matter experts, who were asked to rate how descriptive 135 value statements were of the organisation

Analysis

The Psychologists ensured best practice quantitative and qualitative research methods were used to objectively analyse the data, as described by Breakwell et al., 2012.

Regarding the focus groups and interviews, each statement was assigned a code according to its meaning. Groups of similar codes were then clustered into themes. Themes were aligned to the capabilities described in the organisation's Leadership Capability Framework. For the questionnaires, mean scores were calculated and a ranking system was used to identify the most important leadership qualities. A ranking system was also applied to identify 'highly,' 'moderately' and 'not at all' descriptive statements of the culture. Findings were then integrated to ensure the evidence converged.

Tool Design

An iterative design process was used. Primary stakeholders were consulted on all key decisions and numerous rounds of feedback were incorporated.

- For the culture match, lists of 'highly,' 'moderately' and 'not at all' descriptive statements were organised into 47 triads. These formed the basis of the culture questionnaire. Input was sought on the groupings and the language. A concurrent validation study was then conducted.
- For the cognitive ability tests, computer adaptive tests were chosen to reduce seat time. A low cut off was used to minimise potential for Adverse Impact and so they only filtered out the least able applicants. And a relevant FMCG norm group was selected.
- For the leadership preference questionnaire, the traits identified as key for the role were circulated for input. Feedback was used

to refine the choice of traits and 'ideal' profile. A concurrent validation study was then conducted.

- For the Assessment Centres, concept sheets for each exercise were created. These were circulated for comment and views collated and incorporated. The final exercises were trialled and changes made based on trial feedback.

Training

A train-the-trainer (TTT) methodology was selected to support a global roll out. A series of recorded webinars covered each of the assessment tools, an introduction to assessment, and Assessors' skills. A three-day training course was also delivered to the global heads of Talent for cascade in their regions. The TTT training included:

- Background to the project
- The organisational imperative for change
- Review and discussion of webinar content
- Use of the leadership preference questionnaire
- Practising Assessor skills
- Mock Assessment Centre exercises trial
- TTT toolkit review, including facilitator guide, slides, etc.
- Facilitation skills
- Deployment planning

Outcome

Culture Match

A representative sample of job incumbents completed the Culture Match questionnaire and provided self-ratings of employee engagement. Results showed that where candidate responses were aligned with the organisation's values, employee engagement was significantly higher ($r = 0.31$, $p<0.001$, $n=197$). Consequently, the Practitioners felt confident that candidates that scored higher on the culture match were more likely to be engaged.

This was appreciated by the Global Head of Direct Recruitment Operations who observed, "In designing the Culture Match, it was vital that we not only selected those that share the organisation's values but also that we embrace the unique differences people bring, which taken together enable us to build a strong, rich and diverse organisation."

Cognitive Ability Tests

IBM Workforce Science cognitive ability tests were deployed and widely validated; they consistently showed a statistically significant positive correlation with job performance.

Leadership Preference Questionnaire

A concurrent validity study was used to establish the relationship between the 'ideal' personality profile for leaders and performance in role. Statistically significant correlations were found between both the 'ideal' profile and overall performance ratings ($r = 0.17$, $p<0.001$, n=317) and between individual traits and Leadership Capabilities. For instance, 'achievement orientation' was positively correlated with leadership capability 'Drives own results' ($r=0.22$, $p<0.001$, n=317). Consequently, The Practitioners were confident that candidates who were aligned with the 'ideal' profile were more likely to perform better in the role. The 'ideal' leadership profile also had considerable face validity with stakeholders.

The client reported, "The insights from this tool really allow us to drill into the preferences individuals have and how they align with the demands of the role. This gives us a great insight into not only whether they can do the job but also whether they have future potential as a leader."

Assessment Centre Exercises

All Assessment Centre exercises were thoroughly piloted with job incumbents. A full day mock Assessment Centre (AC) was run and feedback sought from both Assessors and candidates.

Feedback was positive. The client noted, "The AC exercises place candidates in scenarios that are realistic to our organisation at an appropriate level of difficulty for the role they are applying for. They not only enable accurate assessment of the Leadership Capabilities but also provide a positive candidate experience, with people finding them stretching yet fair."

Training

The webinar and train the trainer sessions equipped the Heads of Talent from each region to upskill recruiters, administrators and

Human Resources business partners to roll out the new selection tools.

As a final exercise during the training course, each delegate had an opportunity to say how they were feeling about the project. The client reported, "Universally, people expressed excitement and pride at being involved in a world-class direct recruitment project, felt confident and equipped to deliver the training and were positioned to ensure the tools were used and accepted. They also felt the tools would significantly enhance our talent brand by providing an objective, fair and rigorous assessment."

Overall Achievement of Objectives

The client reflected on the work of the Business Psychologists once the assessment solutions had been deployed. He observed, "Whilst it is too early in deployment of the new approach to report on organisational metrics, we anticipate step change in: (1)   Candidate attraction – measured through talent brand indices and benchmarked against peer organisations, (2) Quality of hire – measured through performance and potential assessments as well as line manager surveys, (3) New hire retention – measured pre and post deployment, (4) Time to productivity – measured pre and post deployment.

"We have achieved our objective of developing a global recruitment process that is applicable to all future organisational leaders from across functions, in 13 languages. We have also reinforced our talent brand with assessments aligned to the capabilities that we consider vital for our leaders."

Acknowledgements

Dilip Boury, Business Psychologist

Robert Blanda, Global Head of Talent Acquisition

International, by Design

Overview

Many organisations that have operations in multiple countries may prefer to use a unified assessment approach. But many assessments have been designed in a country or region, without taking a significant level of diversity into account.

What does it take to create a truly international tool? The team at Cubiks, who developed PAPI 3 to address this need, have shared their story.

Challenge

Organisations around the world had been using Cubiks' Personality and Preference Inventory (PAPI™) for a half-century. Over the years the tool had evolved in line with their shifting needs and changes in working environments.

Given the reality of modern workplaces becoming increasingly globalised, with many individuals working across borders on a daily basis and international organisations seeking to use the same tool across the globe, they felt it was critical that their tools be truly internationally relevant and applicable.

They observed that many personality questionnaires find their roots in the USA or UK – including the original version of PAPI. In the past, to use PAPI outside these territories, they had gone through the steps of translation, back-translation and cultural adaptation. Now they felt that this approach had limitations in the sense that it always meant adapting an inherently UK-centric tool. So, when considering 'what's next,' the Psychometric Designers wanted to address two increasingly important considerations:

- International relevance
- Interactive usage

Psychometric and technical experts developed PAPI 3 preserve PAPI's tried and tested core elements and years of research, by combining history with the latest technology.

The Practitioners found that developing personality scales and their associated items can result in unexpected interpretations, when they are examined across cultures and languages. Some scales in the original PAPI questionnaire even caused problems in certain cultures. For example, they received feedback suggesting:

- In India, the word 'control' had a negative connotation, whereas the words 'influence' or 'assert' were more acceptable
- In France, the words 'influence' and 'control' were associated with manipulation, whereas the phrases 'being responsible for others' or 'being in charge of others' were preferable

When developing PAPI 3, the Practitioners' challenge was how they could tackle this limitation in an innovative way, and deliver an assessment tool that their clients could rely upon to provide the same interpretations and elicit the same calibre of behavioural evidence, in any part of the world. Construct and criterion-related validity data across languages were required to demonstrate this.

The second challenge faced by the Designers was around reporting options. They believed that the market was filled with paper-based reports that were hard to interpret, and not particularly engaging or innovative. They felt that the ideal balance of offering highly insightful content in an engaging and aesthetically attractive way had not yet been achieved. And they found their clients were used to accessing information rapidly and expected the interface to be engaging. Their clients were highly capable of navigating complex online information themselves, so the question was how the Practitioners could leverage their assessment software and transform the visual elements of the PAPI 3 report into an interactive and dynamic portal for consumers.

Approach

The design process for PAPI 3 involved teams from 15 different countries, to help ensure the tool would be fundamentally international in orientation. This design process and implementation took over three years to complete and was carried out in stages. These are described below.

Research and Consultation

- Research and consultation of users and consultants across the globe to produce initial scale concepts
- Confirmed concepts were then reviewed by teams in ten countries which the Business Psychologists believed were broadly representative of PAPI's international usage pattern (China,

Denmark, Finland, France, India, the Netherlands, Poland, Spain, UAE and the UK). This ensured three key things:

- The concept underlying each scale or dimension existed in the relevant language and culture
- It would be acceptable for work-related assessment to measure each concept in the relevant language and culture
- The example personality items and questions produced would be suitable and appropriate for use in the relevant language and culture

Content Creation

- The writing of the personality items and questions involved extensive international collaboration
- Country teams worked on this project in pairs, which had been carefully selected to maximise the differences between the languages of those working together

Trial

- The first trial involved identifying scales and items to include in PAPI 3
  - The items were tested on a sample of 1,186 individuals across five languages: Chinese, Dutch, English, Finnish and French
  - To enhance the validity information for the tool, the trial participants were also invited to complete the Revised NEO Personality Inventory
- The second trial involved gathering cross-cultural validity data and create language specific norms
  - This study was conducted across eleven different languages: Danish, Dutch, English (UK), English (US), Finnish, French, German, Norwegian, Polish, Spanish and Swedish
  - The Consultants observed that good reliability evidence was demonstrated overall, and across the individual language samples
  - For the validity element, individuals were also asked to complete a multi-rater assessment (MRA) which included two colleagues independently rating their performance against a range of work-related competencies. Data was collected for 929 individuals

Report Design

The original idea of the interactive and dynamic report functionality stemmed from a Cubiks Consultant who presented his idea to the PAPI 3 steering group using a mock-up in PowerPoint. The concept to make the exploration of the assessment more interactive and innovative was well received.

The brief for the Cubiks technical team included the following:

- Interactive 'touch-based' explorations of the PAPI profile
- Display text from several different reports
- Visually appealing, engaging and fun, offering a different experience to the user
- Works in major browsers and tablets

In close cooperation with the Research and Development team, they developed a prototype that was still based upon the 'old' version of PAPI. This prototype was showcased to all staff at the Cubiks International Conference, which triggered feedback and new ideas, for example: that it should work offline, present linkages between dimensions, and accommodate branding. The actual build of the solution, working within the 'Cubiks Online' platform, started a year later. The process used was quite agile, although the team felt it was best described as organic, as the business was consulted on a regular basis and feedback was often incorporated in newer versions of the functionality.

Outcome

The Cubiks team believed that internationally relevant and applicable assessment tools were essential for increasingly globalised workplaces.

Reliabilities and validation evidence from the combined language data gave support for the applicability of the PAPI 3 structure and scales in international settings.

Successful Validation

Welsh, Tate & Mortenson, 2015, reported impressive outcomes of the research effort.

Predictions were made by four Psychologists as to which PAPI 3 scales would correlate with which aspects of the NEO PI-R. The results (N = 1,007) showed that all 50 of the predicted relationships were significant, and all the relationships were in the expected direction, with a median of 0.38.

A concurrent validation study was conducted on a combined language sample (N = 929), with a 360° feedback tool measuring performance across 22 representative competency areas as the criterion. Data was collected across 11 different languages: Danish, Dutch, English (UK),

English (US), Finnish, French, German, Norwegian, Polish, Spanish and Swedish.

Prior to the analysis being conducted, two Psychologists independently made predictions about the relationships between the PAPI 3 scales and the competencies. The individual Psychologists' predictions were discussed and a final set of 23 moderate-to-strong hypothesised relationships, and 22 weak hypothesised relationships, were agreed.

When analysed against the other ratings (e.g. line manager, peer, direct report etc.), the results showed that 20 of the 23 predicted moderate-to-strong correlations were significant at the $p < 0.01$ level in the expected direction, and one was significant at the $p < 0.05$ level in the expected direction, with a median correlation of 0.396. All the 22 predicted weak correlations were significant at the $p < 0.01$ level and in the expected direction, with a median correlation of 0.331.

Lessons Learned

Whilst the cross-cultural development process was resource-intensive, and it was challenging for the Consultants to collect adequate data samples across the multiple languages, the benefits of this approach can be seen.

The Cubiks team found that the development of PAPI 3, and the multicultural dimension, drew a lot of interest from within the industry. The Developers shared their view on learning points that can be taken from the development process, including:

- There is value in getting upfront agreement of scale concepts across a range of countries prior to item writing
- It is useful to provide clear item-writing guidelines to all item writers
- It is valuable to collect data from multiple language samples to determine the underlying structure of the tool

After the launch of PAPI 3, many Cubiks clients quickly converted to the newest version. Users working with PAPI 3 and its interactive and dynamic reporting function received it with enthusiasm, and feedback was very positive. Users have expressed that they especially appreciated how effective and engaging the solution is, especially when facilitating virtual feedback sessions, for example when using screen sharing functionality.

A demonstration of the Interactive & Dynamic Reporting tool is available online at: https://www.youtube.com/watch?v=lRKpChZ457c

Acknowledgements

Charlotte Dawson, Cubiks Ltd

Nina Baum, Country Manager, Cubiks UK

Section Three:
Employee Assessment

In this section we look at examples of employee assessment. The use of structured, objective assessments to gain insight into an organisation's talent is not as common as it could be, considering the value it can deliver. And that is demonstrated in these case studies.

First, we see how the military have used innovative assessment tools to identify in-service personnel who have the latent potential to perform well in Cyber roles.

Next, we look at one of the UK's largest employers, the Civil Service. They created a completely bespoke item bank for multimedia assessment, used across the entire Civil Service. The Business Psychologists who met this challenge helped improve the Civil Service and save taxpayers' money.

Third we learn from Regus and their journey through hypergrowth. As their organisation accelerated to achieve growth at eight times previous levels, their Human Resources teams took bold and decisive steps to support the organisation in acquiring and retaining the best talent.

Then we turn attention to Assessors, individuals who play a significant part in recruitment, appraisal, promotion and other processes. This study, applying Interpretative Phenomenological Analysis, produced interesting findings for organisations' reflection, in training and instructing Assessors in various contexts.

Moving on from Assessors to assessing an Executive population. The Chief Executive Officer of a struggling charity wanted to better understand and manage his own and his team's performance and applied Business Psychology provided meaningful insights to act upon.

Penultimately we look at an organisation suffering from a crisis of trust, and their response in the form of a Culture Health Assessment. Find out how they developed a solution to surface early warning signs of risk.

We conclude this section with a case from Rank Group PLC who retained Business Psychologists to help them implement an objective and robust methodology to assess 'high potential' employees, to create a leadership pipeline for the future. Find out how they addressed the Executive Board's perspective on talent within Rank Group.

Cyber Talent Spotting

Overview

The UK's Ministry of Defence (MoD) is experienced in addressing all sorts of challenges. When facing a new enemy, in the form of cyber security risk, they acted fast to find innovative and sustainable solutions.

They chose to apply Business Psychology to grow their capabilities in cyber defence: to identify in-service personnel who had the latent potential to perform well in Cyber roles and the motivation to continue in those roles. This allowed the MoD to target, and get a greater return, on their investment in training their cyber defence teams.

As this case concerns National Security, we cannot share all the details. It nevertheless demonstrates the value of psychology applied to tough talent challenges.

Challenge

Significant Constraints

Typically, when an organisation requires talent with a specialised skillset, they look to the market for those skills. The MoD do not usually have that luxury; they recruit internally, literally from within their own ranks. Existing personnel need to be redeployed, to learn new things and address emerging needs. And the military have far less flexibility to increase pay or incentivise and retain staff than the private sector enjoys.

The MoD is in competition with the private sector for skilled Cyber individuals and relies on people motivated to serve their country, to remain in service.

Training budgets were a factor too. The MoD needed to find people for Cyber roles who had the ability to learn the job quickly and become high performers who would enjoy the niche roles within Cyber Defence.

To make this challenge even tougher, there was no blueprint for cyber recruitment across the various roles within their Cyber Defence operations. Few organisations in the world had identified the distinctive characteristics of successful cyber specialists at this time, let alone found ways to assess individuals' latent potential to learn to do the work. And the MoD were seeing high levels of turnover in the roles.

So, the challenge was to identify individuals from the Army, Royal Air Force and Royal Navy:

- with the capacity to learn quickly to operate effectively in cyber roles
- who had a predisposition for cyber work, so that they would thrive and last in these jobs

Finally, military cultural considerations introduced additional novel challenges. This needed to be done within unusually rigid posting processes, in a rapidly developing career field within the military, and a rank-agnostic working environment.

Psychologists' Dilemma

The Business Psychologists engaged to address this requirement for the MoD, from IBM's Workforce Science team, had many years of experience working with the military. Even so, they found this uniquely challenging.

A paradox to be addressed throughout the project was the concept of 'good' in the military, versus the reality of being 'good' in Cyber. For example:

- In a military hierarchy, rank supersedes ability. Cyber roles required individual skill to take precedence, leading to conflict with tradition
- Individuals were allocated to tasks in accordance with the military posting statement "the needs of the service come first, those of the individual a close second." In this context genuine talent was often overlooked
- The military emphasises dynamic, physical characteristics in contrast with a more sedentary Cyber approach

These constraints reduced the number of people in service who were suitable for work in the demanding, high-skill Cyber environment.

The Psychologists needed to design a solution which offered the best value for tax-payers' money whilst overcoming very specific challenges:

- Assessing aptitude rather than existing knowledge and ability

- The need specifically was to find a way to identify latent Cyber aptitude as opposed to the presence of learned skills
- Security restrictions
  - Security considerations were paramount which would impact access to existing Cyber specialists working in the military and information they could (or more usually could not) share about their roles, making job analysis particularly difficult
- Clear output
  - The outcomes of the processes needed to be clear; there was a need for robust, easily interpreted results, in a format suited to a military audience

Approach

The range of unique challenges presented by the MoD's requirement became even more apparent once the project kicked-off. Flexibility and innovation were essential to ensure valid scientific methods could be applied to deliver a solution.

The Psychologists and their MoD stakeholders agreed the solution would take the form of a suite of assessments for latent cyber ability, subsequently referred to as the Defence Cyber Aptitude Test (DCAT).

The design phases included:

- Job analysis
- Existing test item trialling
- Customisation and re-norming
- New content development
- DCAT trial
- Analysis and refinement
- Final technical build (for online administration)
- Roll-out and subsequent build of an additional assessment and re-norm of DCAT

Job Analysis

For job analysis, 27 one-to-one interviews and eight focus groups were conducted with a representative sample. The sensitive nature of the roles hampered typical job analysis by restricting what details could be shared. The Psychologists adjusted to these limitations. They projected transcript notes during focus groups to demonstrate transparency, encourage participation and engender trust. And, in many cases, they relied on analogies to establish required skills, abilities and working environments.

The constructs identified as relevant across all roles were accuracy, systematic approach, logic, fault finding and aptitude for working with code.

Existing Test Item Trialling

IBM's original proposition was to keep the cost of the project down by leveraging existing cognitive ability assessment content. They planned to evaluate IBM's extensive off-the-shelf personality preference traits library, Kenexa Personality Assessment (KPA), for use. They had also previously developed the Army Cognitive Test (ACT), for British Army recruitment, so that was going to be trialled as well.

However, there was a concern that the applicant pools for the original British Army recruitment and Joint Forces Cyber purposes would be so disparate that the cognitive assessments would need augmentation, if not complete replacement.

Initial assessment trials conducted with focus group participants and interviewees identified that 'Cyber potential' assessment required a more in-depth assessment of personnel than the existing assessments would provide.

The team kept the numerical and verbal reasoning elements of the ACT. Whilst the original rationale behind these tools was to create something accessible to a population with a more diverse range of abilities, their Computer Adaptive Testing (CAT) format made them suitable for use here too.

The norm established by the initial trial population (n = 262) was more leptokurtic and negatively skewed than the existing norm. As such, whilst Cyber candidates would take the same assessment as used elsewhere, the CAT approach results in them being exposed to a different area of the item bank (higher level items).

Novel Test Design

A team of Psychometric Assessment Designers came together to create this solution. The team created two Cyber specific ability tests which between them assessed accuracy, systematic approach, logic, fault finding and aptitude for working with code.

In their research, they found no reference to these constructs specifically in existing psychometric literature. The Designers had to create entirely novel assessment question formats to identify these abilities.

Accuracy is generally assessed under time constraints, but the psychologists felt that approach could contaminate other constructs with an irrelevant requirement. Instead, the Designers developed an assessment which measured accuracy through application of a systematic approach rather than under time pressure.

To assess fault finding and working with code, the Designers created a pictorial code which would give no benefit to individuals with previous coding experience, having established early on that they needed to assess for latent cyber aptitude, rather than existing programming skills. Ultimately, an individual's interest and ability to continuously learn new products was far more important than attaining expert user level in any single programming language.

Many of the personality preferences identified as aligned to the role were counter-intuitive and sat outside of typical 'service' ethos. For example, individuals with strong preference for persevering with tasks until completion might find it challenging to cease work, or hand over a task, with no tangible completion point. Therefore, 'good fit' bands were developed and tailored accordingly.

During job analysis, an exercise developed by the existing Cyber personnel was presented to the design team. They adapted this content to create a Situational Judgement Test (SJT), but trialling did not return favourable results for selection purposes. However, they felt that it did give useful insights into the Cyber roles, and so they determined it useful as a Realistic Job Preview (RJP). The Designers then created a more traditional style of SJT in collaboration with a representative group of intelligence analysts.

Outcome

The Practitioners initially endeavoured to create multiple role-specific assessments, but the job analysis identified a core set of traits and abilities required across them all. The final product therefore consisted of core ability assessments as well as interchangeable options as follows:

– Two generic and two cyber-specific ability tests

- An SJT for intelligence analyst roles; and an unscored RJP for other roles
- A personality preference questionnaire

Norms were based on trials when first released, but the team anticipated that maximum performance assessment means would increase. This accounted for the trial population (incumbents) potentially being be less motivated to perform well without any consequences, and more likely to experience test fatigue as the average seat time for all assessments was 85 minutes (with one individual taking 165 minutes to complete all the items).

Re-norming of the final tool allowed for streamlining the assessment. Most individuals could complete the final assessment suite in less than 50 minutes, or significantly less if not taking the personality preference questionnaire component.

Rigorous validation delivered positive results, but details cannot be shared. However, evidence of the success of the project was the MoD's satisfaction with the work and the strong working relationship built between the Psychologists and their MoD stakeholders. This was evidenced in their ongoing relationship which led to subsequent projects conducted through the first half of the following year. For example:

- Design of a detailed feedback report which enabled Interviewers to conduct a competency-based interview, prompted by fit to the ideal personality preference profile
- Development of an Intelligence Analyst SJT (with a Cronbach's Alpha of 0.637), created in three weeks; the speedy development time was possible thanks to the buy-in established
- Exploration of an open access simulation to act as an attraction tool, as well as an RJP

Acknowledgements

Major Harry Porteous, Defence Cyber Programme Manager, MoD

Trevor Pons, Business Psychologist

Sean Keeley, Managing Consultant and Psychometric Designer, IBM

Jo Parkes, Senior Talent Consultant and Psychometric Designer, IBM

Chiara Staples, Project Manager, IBM

The Civil Service Solution

Overview

The Civil Service is one of the UK's largest employers. Following a Civil-Service-wide consultation, the Government Recruitment Service identified the need to design a completely bespoke item banked multimedia assessment to be available across the entire Civil Service. And, due to the complexity of the scoring, accessibility and technological requirements, an entirely new online assessment architecture needed to be developed.

This is the story of the courageous Business Psychologists who took on this significant challenge, with tight deadlines, and ultimately helped not only improve Civil Service recruitment but also save taxpayers' money.

Challenge

The UK Government Recruitment Service (GRS) took the decision to use psychometric assessment to improve the effectiveness of the Civil Service recruitment process, by identifying the best candidates available.

Following a Civil Service-wide consultation, GRS had identified complex requirements for this work, including:

– The assessment would be based on the existing Civil Service assessment framework of ten competencies

– It would be applicable to all Civil Service departments across six grades of seniority

– Stakeholder involvement was essential to ensuring validity and buy-in

– Psychometric rigour and validity needed to be evidenced

– The assessment needed to be fair and accessible; ideally mobile-first with a practice site to enable all candidates to familiarise themselves with requirements

– The assessment should enhance existing processes, making them more efficient and cost effective

– Tight timescales required high levels of commitment and rigorous project management

– Technology would be required to deliver innovations in tool design and delivery

The GRS chose to work with the Business Psychologists at PSI due to their track record in designing fair and robust assessments, and their desire to design a unique solution that would meet GRS' requirements fully.

From the supplier perspective, reviewing the project challenges, the technological requirements stood out. Due to the complexity and unique nature of the technological, scoring and accessibility requirements, an entirely new online assessment administration platform needed to be developed, within the short four to five months allowed for completion.

Approach

A team of specialists convened to develop a completely bespoke item banked multimedia situational judgement assessment, to be administered online, available across the entire Civil Service.

At the beginning of the project the key stakeholders in the Civil Service and PSI's Design Team had a series of meetings to understand the full requirements for successful delivery. Due to the extensive range of requirements, every activity of the project was scoped out for both sides of the Project Team (i.e. GRS and the Test Designers), and timescales and responsibilities were assigned to each.

Consultation and Development

For the test to be accurate across departments and levels of seniority, relevant situations, tasks and context needed to be identified. To achieve this, 60 deep-dive interviews with SMEs were carried out and over 200 job descriptions were reviewed. From this, a set of 839 tasks were identified and a set of 364 critical incidents were generated.

Based on this job analysis and working with the GRS project lead, a detailed brief of the context, tasks, and common situations was created. A team of nine Psychologists used this to generate a set of 513 scenarios, 3,078 actions, and 280 interview questions. The content was reviewed by 71 internal experts and three Chartered Psychologists. Of the Experts consulted, 42% represented diversity networks or units.

Relevance was a core challenge for the multimedia content and production. To address this, the scripts were reviewed across six half-day workshops with relevant Civil Service stakeholders. Based on this, edits were made and 56 scenarios were dropped. Significant effort was invested in identifying actors, as over 1,300 applications were received. Following detailed review, 57 of the most appropriate actors were cast to cover 77 roles. Across six days, 67 videos depicting work-related scenarios were produced for the assessment item bank.

This work formed the basis of the desired assessment: an item bank of Situational Judgement Test (SJT) items that comprised 44 testlets.

The Design Team utilised best practice research to optimise the fairness of the test. For example, previous research showed a four-point rating format to have the lowest associated subgroup differences. This created a challenge, as item banked SJTs typically use best/worst formats. Therefore, a new approach to item banked SJT scoring was developed using the Rasch model.

The Designers elected to use the Rasch approach to scoring. Rasch analysis is a statistical procedure within item response theory (IRT) that calculates item difficulty in relation to personal ability and weights the overall scores accordingly. The resulting scores are on a linear scale, allowing easy comparison of measures and easy interpretation of changes in scores.

Assessment content was trialled with over 4,000 Civil Service employees, resulting in 6,371 completions of trial versions of the test. To ensure sufficient data was collected to implement the Rasch approach to scoring, an additional 10,000 completions were collected from external participants. Therefore, over 16,000 participants were used to collect sufficient data for developing the norms, determining item difficulties, construct validity and to inform Adverse Impact analysis.

Inclusive and Accessible

The Civil Service is committed to the Disability Confident scheme. They aim to lead the way in creating a disability-inclusive culture where colleagues can realise their full potential, with recruitment processes accessible to all.

So, the Project Team included a diverse range of stakeholders at every stage in the test design. Representatives from 13 different diversity networks were involved and influenced every stage of the test's development. Seventy-one experts were asked to assess and comment on the fairness/inclusivity of the test content and over 800 Black, Asian and minority ethnic (BAME) Civil Servants were involved in trialling.

GRS made a significant effort throughout the project to include disabled people in the scoping, implementation and early testing phases. The Digital Accessibility Centre was commissioned to test the assessment software to ensure it met best practice accessibility standards and legislation. This testing involved 10 Quality Assurers covering a range of user types. The software met the standard and the team responded to additional advice on further work that could be done.

Accelerated Delivery

Due to the extensive requirements and short timescales this was a significant undertaking from a stakeholder engagement and project management perspective, requiring both organisations to work very collaboratively. This included bi-weekly calls with the GRS project lead during the content development phase and required daily calls with the Civil Service HR Digital Team during the software implementation phase.

Outcome

Within the first 16 months, the test was completed by over 170,000 candidates in the recruitment process, as well as 90,000 job seekers using the practice site. In that time, the test helped inform hiring decisions for over 1,200 job vacancies from administrative to leadership roles.

Relevant and Accurate

Overall feedback was positive. This was reflected by the significant adoption of the assessment by 41 departments across the Civil Service.

Analysis showed that candidates' test scores were predictive of performance at interview (N=4,301) and being offered a job (N=37,751).

Updates were continually implemented with new video scenarios being added, and additional analysis based on 167,664 candidates' data was used to enhance the accuracy of the test.

Inclusive and Accessible

Overall inclusivity, fairness and accessibility were a high priority. The project involved significant stakeholder involvement with contributors from 27 professions, 98 departments and agencies, staff networks, the Civil Service Commissioner's office and Trade Unions. Based on the analysis of a sample of 58,295 candidates, the test was deemed fair at the test's pass mark and did not cause Adverse Impact for candidates with disabilities, BAME status, or LGBT (lesbian, gay, bisexual, and transgender) status.

The software was tested again by the Digital Accessibility Centre to ensure that the test met WCAG 2.0 AA standard. The software was enhanced further and was close to being compliant with WCAG 2.0 AAA standard, the highest accessibility standard. Since the test's deployment the number of requests for adjustments by disabled test takers decreased by 80%.

Accelerated Delivery

The timescales were so tight (five months) that every activity needed to be delivered in short timescales. For example, an average of 34.2 scenarios were written per day; in 13 days 6,371 trial versions of the test were completed by Civil Servants and 122 days of consultants' design time was delivered within a 10-week period.

In the same timeframe, the team of nine software developers and one Quality Assurer had to deliver the new online system, with a sophisticated new scoring approach, mobile-first design and scalable servers. In total, 352 software development days were needed to meet the required standard, which was a significant achievement in the time allowed.

Enhanced Efficiency

Sir Jeremy Heywood, Head of the Civil Service commented "The Civil Service is undergoing big changes in the way it works, to become more efficient and effective in the delivery of services, while responding to some of the biggest challenges in its history." The Business Psychologists believed that this project was a perfect example of delivering against these goals during a challenging time.

They further reported that the Civil Service estimated that the implementation of the test saved c.£550,000 in resources needed to manually sift job applications within a year of release.

For more information about the project, please watch this video: https://vimeo.com/274114473/1a6264cb77

Acknowledgements

Ali Shalfrooshan, Principal Consultant, PSI

Paul Weldon, Principal Occupational Psychologist, Government Recruitment Service

Mary Mescal, Senior Consultant, PSI

Willard Xavier, Quality Analyst, PSI

Andras Gall, Senior Software Developer

Justin Rickard, Senior Software Developer

Lauren Smith, Campaign Delivery Officer, Government Recruitment Services

Mark Williams, Associate Product Manager, Government Recruitment Services

Martin Barnston, Delivery Manager - Civil Service Jobs, Government Recruitment Services

Keith Thomas, Director, Sightline

Ashley Kitchen, Senior Editor, Sightline

Joanne Moncur, Senior Consultant, PSI

Philippa Riley, R&D Director, PSI

Martin Hughes, Software Development Manager, PSI

Rachel Chandler, Resourcing Consultant, PSI

Amy Thompson, Client Services Manager, PSI

Ben Schwencke, Research Specialist, Test Partnership

Lisette Guy, Research Specialist, Test Partnership

Human Resources in Hypergrowth

Overview

During a period of hyper-growth, Regus' Human Resources (HR) team were called upon to deliver a high performing workforce with unprecedented pace and precision. Regus designed and deployed a global recruitment process, underpinned by Business Psychology, for over 100 countries. In so doing the business was enabled to hire effectively to meet demands at a time when growth had accelerated to eight-times previous levels.

The HR team then turned their attention to optimising their workforce. Again, relying on Business Psychology to optimise their workforce, they commenced an ambitious plan to understand individual characteristics in their employees that were related to business success and proactively address learning and development needs. Read more about the bold choices the Human Resources team made to help Regus stay on top!

Challenge

The Executives at Regus found themselves at a crossroads. Their future-forward model, offering office spaces and services for ad hoc use, had been ahead of its time. In the first 20 or so years of operation they had opened on average one new location each week, thus capturing and leading in their market. They invested heavily in innovation and services, to maintain a loyal customer base. Then analysts advised them they were at risk; with hotels, coffee shops and a number of other venues moving into their space, they had a choice: act fast to retain control or lose their lead and possibly their legacy.

They chose to act fast, moving into a phase of hypergrowth, reinventing themselves to retain and maximise their advantage. Within a year they reengineered their organisation, decentralised a number of operations and opened 400 new locations, across 100 countries.

Regus' HR team was at the heart of the transformation; taking tough decisions to enable the business to succeed. Their short-term challenges were clear:

- Decentralise HR services, with the associated considerations for training and enabling regional operators, to increase responsiveness, local accountability and reduce central costs
- Hire, onboard and train managers and service teams for 400 locations, in 100 countries, with minimal or no existing presence
- Ensure sales teams around the world were equipped to increase their delivery to fund these huge investments

Regus' approach to workforce performance management had traditionally been inconsistent. But they grasped this critical opportunity to create a uniform recruitment process.

During this period the HR team recognised the value of applying Business Psychology to workforce decision-making, whilst also investing in increased automation and analytical capabilities, and they commenced a journey to insight-driven HR.

Approach

Decentralised Hiring

A wholesale review of recruitment practices globally was undertaken – in more than 100 territories, across the US, UK, EMEA and APAC – to inform a robust and scalable new way of working. The review involved looking at all areas of recruitment: who did what, why, when, where and how. Interviews were conducted with key stakeholders, budget owners and Directors, whilst surveys were used to get insight from candidates too. The findings were benchmarked against admired companies. Hiring managers, who became aware of the need for change, welcomed help to learn new ways of working.

The inclusion of a predictive psychological assessment, that could be easily incorporated into the recruitment process, was critical to the overall success of the new recruitment approach. As decision-making on candidate selection was to be moved away from a specialist recruiter community, to a broad selection of non-specialist Hiring Managers, there was a need to ensure these non-assessment specialists had tools to guide their recruitment decision-making. This would ensure hiring standards were consistent in terms of Regus' global standards and role requirements.

A new scalable solution for all regions was created which put the power and accountability for hiring in the hands of local business/budget owners (local country General Managers). Regus' global recruitment team created unified standards, policies and processes for all to use, to ensure the quality of the candidate experience was improved as well as the quality of hire, addressing a necessity for Regus' brand to be sustained by new hires.

Regus deployed BrassRing for applicant management, unifying and automating the recruitment process and collecting of relevant data. Within the BrassRing system they deployed custom assessment tools which would quickly and effectively sift candidates based on core preferences and behaviours required to be effective in Regus' jobs and culture. (See more under the heading, "Global Hiring for Hypergrowth.")

As central recruitment teams in each geography were to be dissolved and individual Hiring Managers in each centre given entire accountability for their hiring, IBM Talent Consultants were retained to provide systems and assessment advice to facilitate the necessary changes.

In summary, decentralisation of Regus' recruitment activities was achieved with:

- An applicant tracking system which established and automated a standardised process which was easy to follow
- Robust candidate assessment tools, effectively identifying and filtering out unsuitable candidates with minimal effort
- Associated training, assuring Hiring Managers that candidates progressed to interview were likely to be successful in their roles, and thus justified the investment of the Hiring Managers' time in an interview

At the same time, Regus effectively improved candidates' experiences of recruitment with enhanced employer branding, careers site and toolkits. Candidates could have a clear insight into Regus' value proposition, role requirements and a globally consistent recruitment experience.

Global Hiring for Hypergrowth

Ensuring new Hiring Managers in each territory would be successful in identifying candidates who would succeed in their roles at Regus required input from Business Psychologists. Regus wanted to take a scientific approach to creating a predictive scalable assessment tool, which they worked with Business Psychologists at IBM to deliver. IBM's remit was to reduce Regus' hiring risks, and save them time.

This would be achieved with an automated assessment which selected candidates on the basis of core preferences and behaviours relevant to effectiveness in Regus' jobs and culture.

Psychological models informed the assessment tool created, aligned to Regus' requirement that culture-fit be assessed along with candidates' disposition to succeed at Regus. This was based on research into existing employees' performance and success. The assessment tool IBM created showed how desirable candidates could be identified, to ensure hiring of candidates who were likely to achieve in role performance standards over 50% higher than below average performers.

Assessment Model

IBM Talent Consultants' approach to defining individuals' potential to add value in organisations addressed a combination of innate capacities (what they are naturally inclined and able to do) and learned capability (what they have studied, practiced and experienced). When people also fit the culture of the organisation they are working in; they are likely to deploy their capacities and capabilities most effectively. IBM's approach was aligned to Regus' requirement that culture be assessed along with candidates' innate capacities and behaviours; leaving the assessment of further learned capabilities to the interview stage/Hiring Managers.

Comprehensive Job analysis was carried out using Subject Matter Expert interviews and an open-ended critical incident questionnaire across relevant roles including: Customer Service Representatives (CSRs), Senior Customer Service Representatives (SCSRs) and General Managers (GMs). Performance measures used in validating the research findings included retrospective data from Regus' Performance Appraisal cycle, i.e. (i) Prior Initiatives and Goals, (ii) Regus Success Factors, (iii) Position Success Factors and (iv) Management Success Factors. These were averaged to create a measure of overall performance, subsequently used in all validation analyses.

A single assessment tool was created which could be used to effectively assess candidates being recruited into four different field roles. This approach was unconventional, but validation demonstrated it was a fair and robust option in this case. Additionally, it met Regus' requirement for simplicity.

Prior to deployment, the custom assessment based on critical incidents was trialled with employees in an unsupervised environment with no time limits (a Situational Judgement Test (SJT)). Respondents were presented with items that consisted of written descriptions of likely situations and three options describing possible responses. In each item the respondents were directed to select the response option they thought was the best course of action under the circumstances. Matched assessment and performance data were available on 243 current Regus employees. Of the participants in the concurrent sample who reported demographics: both genders were represented in multiple geographies and ages included employees from 16 to 65 years of various ethnicities.

The assessment results were analysed to determine internal consistency reliability. As SJTs are multi-dimensional, low internal consistency reliability is expected. Appropriately, an Alpha coefficient of 0.3 was measured. A Factor Analysis was then conducted to determine the competencies measured and an appropriate distribution was found with each of Regus' seven priority behaviours all occurring in multiple instances. SJT items were correlated with the criteria in the validation sample. The final SJT was derived by summing the most valid 15 items from the full situational judgment predictor. The tool provided assessment outcomes which proved predictive of in-role performance/success. Two post-deployment Adverse Impact analyses showed the test to be performing without discriminating against particular groups.

Sales Team Optimisation

Regus' HR team recognised that optimisation of their sales function was business critical. To facilitate this, they identified two employee populations for attention, the Inside Sales team (approximately 500 employees) and the General Managers who manage the Regus sites (approximately 2,000 employees).

HR's plan of action was:

- Engage the Sales Director in order to obtain support to work with the seller population, then engage the sales population in the initiative
- Assess a representative sample of the existing sales population to measure preferences and abilities, correlating this to their sales

performance, to establish critical characteristics that were associated with successful sales performance within Regus

- Use the insights gathered to create a Learning Needs Analysis to inform the training and development interventions and investments that would be most likely to deliver a return on these investments in sellers
- Use the insights gathered to create a customised recruitment assessment approach to ensure future hiring efforts were focused on those candidates most likely to succeed at Regus
- Gain Executive support and funding to expand the exploration of the workforce at this in-depth level, to further inform business decisions about talent management, development and succession planning

At this time Regus' concurrent validation of their Customer Service assessment had demonstrated strong results. (See more under the heading, "Global Hiring for Hypergrowth.") For example, they could predict levels of performance on the basis of personal characteristics; those identified as 'above average' in their assessment achieved performance ratings from their managers approximately 25% higher than the majority of their peers. But that would not be enough. Whilst valid and useful, that metric did not speak to the Sales Director's key metrics, 'hard numbers.' For this reason, the HR team introduced sales performance data into the assessment analysis done with this population.

Assessment Model

The HR team won support for funding from the Sales Director by illustrating how other organisations had benefited from using psychometric assessments to inform salesforce hiring and deployment.

With the Sales Director's commitment, the HR team gained access to relevant business metrics against which to measure business impact in each population, both Inside Sellers and General Managers. IBM then set about gathering information on these individuals' characteristics, their working styles, abilities and preferences. This was done through the administration of a composite online psychometric assessment which measured factors that had been proven to correlate to successful sales performance in many organisations including: cognitive ability, situational judgment, detail orientation, initiative, persistence and other factors.

The Inside Seller and General Manager populations' support of this initiative was won by clear communications regarding the intentions of the programme along with a commitment to giving the individuals access to their assessment results with developmental guidance.

Validation

Regus supplied IBM with data regarding each Inside Seller's performance using seven business metrics, including opportunity-to-conversion rates on key products and total sales revenue values. GM performance was defined using further business metrics including Net Promoter Scores, earnings figures and employee engagement data.

IBM then analysed the data collected to identify characteristics which:

- most significantly correlated to sales success (positive)
- most significantly correlated to poor performance (negative)
- occurred most prevalently in the sales population and how they were distributed

To support development, and return value on their investment, Regus could use this insight to create training and developmental interventions.

Regus' HR team, having confidence in the clarity and relevance of the findings, then presented back to the business all that had been found. This met the business' need for a clear success profile, against which to hire and develop sellers, and a compelling learning needs analysis to justify necessary investments to improve sales performance.

This early success was sufficient to gain Executive support and funding to expand the exploration of the workforce at this in-depth level to further inform business decisions about talent management, development and succession planning. The HR team were given the remit to assess all the Country Managers and Area Directors in Regus globally to similarly find ways to target developmental interventions to optimise their performance.

Outcome

Determined effort on the part of the HR team paid off. Within two years, great gains had been made. Based on behavioural assessments and concurrent validation studies, demonstrating relationships between individual characteristics and 'hard' business metrics, they understood the individual characteristics that related to effective performance across approximately 80% of their workforce. These insights allowed for improved effectiveness in recruitment, learning, development, succession planning and promotion decisions which Regus' leaders continue to benefit from.

"We have received additional sponsorship and investment from our Executives who recognise the value of having facts and figures to demonstrate the quality of their workforce. We are able to show them where they have talent and where they have risks, what portion of the population are performing well and could be further developed, who is exceeding expectations and may be ready for a bigger challenge and, in contrast, which individuals appear to be a poor fit for the roles that they're in." – *Francesca Peters, Chief Talent Officer, Regus Group*

Decentralised Hiring

Within three months of project commencement, the new approach went live in the UK and USA, with a total of 74 countries' operations aligning to the new approach within the following six months. Deployment continued with translation of tools into 12 languages so that adoption reached all 100 countries within a further six months. A poll of Hiring Managers' experience indicated 71% did not think anything could have been done better to ease their transition.

Post deployment, IBM conducted quarterly reviews of the assessment data collected as more geographies commenced use of the assessment. Psychologists demonstrated that the assessments in use continued to perform as anticipated, with no unacceptable Adverse Impact. Although the use of an online assessment was new to Hiring Managers, post deployment polls reflected positive feedback from Hiring Manager on the screening process.

A year after initial deployment almost 20,000 applications had been received, around 7,000 progressed beyond application questions and SJT assessment stage, and 700 individuals were hired. Additionally, a talent pool of around 3,000 'live' candidates was created; these candidates were preselected but not yet offered roles (waiting on appropriate vacancies to become available and an offer can then be extended).

Local Hiring Managers also demonstrated greater confidence in the recruitment and assessment process by becoming less reliant on the use of agency temps (resulting in cost savings).

The final assessment delivered was significantly related to the Regus' overall performance scores (r = .21) demonstrating predictive validity. The correlations between the components of performance and the overall predictor were all positive and most reached statistical significance. All of these validity estimates were also reported corrected, as correlations were likely to be biased downward due to range restriction and criterion unreliability.

The trial sample was divided into three groups, i.e. scores on the SJT which were below average (bottom 25%), average (middle 50%) and above average (top 25%). There were useful differences in mean performance across the three groups. Those in the above average group of the predictor were rated approximately 25.4% higher than those in the average group and 53% higher than those in the below average group for overall performance. The final assessment had a raw validity coefficient of .21 which was corrected for unreliability to .27. A validity coefficient of .27 can be interpreted as an 18% increase in "hits" with scores at the 50th percentile. ("Hits" are recommended candidates most likely to be above average hires.)

In summary, Regus confidently used the objective psychology-based assessment in filtering candidates in the recruitment process, knowing that it would enable them to hire a higher quality of staff, i.e. identifying those most likely to be successful in context of the particular demands of the field roles in Regus.

Candidates could be assured of fair assessment, in an easy to understand online format, with assessment questions based on Regus' clear understanding of role demands.

Sales Team Optimisation

The HR Team achieved their objective of demonstrating the value of using an insight into human behaviour to inform business decisions which would increase business success.

They were able to demonstrate various relationships between characteristics in the seller populations and business performance. Some findings may have been intuitive, such as seeing relationships between a preference for influencing and higher net promoter scores, between persistence and detail orientation and earnings, or cognitive ability and sales. Nevertheless, having quantified the extent of the effect that these characteristics could have, in which settings, for example, some differed by geography or product, meant that Regus could make informed decisions about how they identified and developed these characteristics in their workforce.

Over 60% of the 'Seller' population gave their time to complete the comprehensive assessments. In spontaneous feedback participants described it as "very impressive" and "informative." The Learning Need Analysis which was created at both a group and individual level, provided:

- HR and the Sales Director insight into where and how to focus training and development interventions and investments
- Information for the individuals who took part in the assessment on how they should focus their developmental efforts to improve their performance outcomes

Regus were able to define a custom assessment approach for use in future recruitment of Inside Sellers and General Managers.

And Regus' Executives have started to recognise the value of creating deeper insights into their workforce and have supported the HR team in undertaking additional analysis, including in their most senior Operational Leaders: their Country Managers and Area Directors.

Acknowledgements

Charlotte Harris, Global HR Director, Regus Group

Nick Mayes, Analytics Leader, Regus Group

Marija Potter, Business Psychologist and Managing Talent Consultant, IBM

Caroline Fortunski, Business Psychologist and Senior Talent Consultant, IBM

Chiara Staples, Project Manager, IBM

Assessor Impact

Overview

Assessors are often used in recruitment, appraisal, promotion and other processes. And yet studies suggest the majority of companies believe that lenient appraisals jeopardise the validity of their appraisal systems. The impact that a particular Assessor may have on the outcome for the Assessee (the Subject of the assessment) thus warrants attention.

In this innovative Masters research project, Interpretative Phenomenological Analysis was used to isolate the differences between more and less lenient Assessors. Whilst the Assessor group was small so the findings need to be considered in that context, all organisations using Assessors could usefully reflect on the research findings.

Challenge

Matthew Atkinson identified a consistent finding in business, that some Assessors were systematically more lenient than others. Recognising the potentially significant implications of this fact, he decided to address this in a research project.

Background

Research suggested that 'leniency' was first used in reference to assessment in 1929, when Assessors were found to rate well above the midpoint of the scale used.

The issue of Assessor leniency remained an area of research in the academic community since then and had been referred to as the 'hawk-dove effect.'

This leniency effect has been found to be independent from other types of Assessor inaccuracy, including the halo effect.

To combat this leniency effect, some organisations implement forced ranking procedures whereby the population of Assessors, such as performance managers, can only award the top ratings to a pre-defined percentage of Subjects. But forced ranking has been widely maligned, so organisations are justified in looking for better solutions.

Additionally, as Assessors are used in several activities associated with the study and practice of Business Psychology, factors in the effectiveness of Assessor activity stood out as a topic of research was important in the field.

Possible Explanations

It can be said that previous research has failed to unearth the **cause** of the leniency effect, and it is therefore difficult for organisations to control. Previous research had indicated:

- The link between leniency and Assessor personality was weak and unclear
  - Agreeableness might be associated with leniency in some contexts, but findings were inconsistent; and
  - Conscientiousness might be associated with severity in some contexts, but findings were inconsistent
- There was no robust link between leniency and the cognitive ability of Assessors

Research into Motivational factors – such as Assessors having hidden agendas, friendships with Subjects or being driven by conflict avoidance – had dried up over a decade before, with little notable progress having been made since.

Research Constraints

The Researcher observed that almost all studies to investigate the leniency effect had been conducted in laboratory, not organisational, settings. It would therefore be difficult to apply existing research directly to the practitioner community.

It could be argued that the scarcity of organisational, as opposed to laboratory, studies was because of the impracticalities of identifying and studying 'lenient' or 'severe' Assessors within business contexts. Firstly, the terms 'severe' and 'lenient' are both relative terms, inextricably linked to a comparison group. Second, to identify 'severe' Assessors within an organisational context, it would be necessary to compare inherently subjective Assessor ratings with a parallel objective assessment of Subjects. The nature of Assessor-based assessment however is such that a like for like comparison would not be easily achieved. Afterall, if it were possible to objectively identify strong candidates without Assessors, organisations would have little need to employ them.

Approach

Research Subjects

The Researcher found an organisational partner to work with, to carry out his research, and proposed taking an interpretative phenomenological approach to analysing a group of their Assessors.

Conducting this study in an organisational setting enhanced its business relevance but necessitated some sensitivity too. For example, subjective descriptors for Assessors, like 'lenient' and 'harsh,' needed to be avoided.

Working with a small group of Assessors, he distinguished between:

- Assessors who could be described as having a "low propensity to reject," with a track record of rejecting ≤ 7% of candidates they assessed; and
- Assessors who could be described as having a "propensity to reject," with a track record of rejecting ≥17% of candidates assessed

In the research group:

- All Assessors had completed 25 or more assessments
- No Assessors had rejected between 7% and 17% of Subjects

He thus commenced his work differentiating between Assessors with a Propensity to Reject (PR), aka Hawks, and Assessors with a Low Propensity to Reject (LPR), aka Doves.

Research Steps

The Researcher began by investigating the underlying beliefs, assumptions and motivations of Assessors, in order to understand how Assessors with differing propensities to reject candidates conceptualised their roles as Assessors.

Interpretative Phenomenological Analysis (IPA) was used for two main reasons:

- There was a need to investigate individuals' own understanding of their role as Assessors, so qualitative (rather than quantitative) analytical methodology was appropriate. A quantitative approach could potentially mask the richness of the information shared by participants about their attitudes and beliefs.

- Of the different methodologies available, IPA stood out to the Researcher for its strong epistemological alignment to the research question

After conducting semi-structured interviews with each Assessor, transcripts were interrogated in line with IPA methodology (analysing the words used, and the researcher's experience in the interview itself).

Three superordinate themes were established, showing differences in how PR and LPR groups conceptualized their roles as Assessors. These themes were:

- Core Purpose
  - PR conceptualization: providing a service to a business
  - LPR conceptualization: providing help to an individual
- Attitude
  - PR conceptualization: exerting one's self
  - LPR conceptualization: experiencing someone else
- Doubt
  - PR conceptualization: forming one's view
  - LPR conceptualization: doubting one's self

In summary, it was observed that lenient Assessors tended to believe their purpose was to provide help to an individual, whereas less lenient Assessors believed their purpose was to provide a service to a business. Further, lenient Assessors' attitudes were more passive than less lenient Assessors' attitudes. Finally, lenient Assessors expressed more doubt than did less lenient Assessors.

Outcome

Applying the Insight

Demonstrating that 'lenient' and 'severe' Assessors conceptualized their roles differently, trainers can set expectations and clarify roles before assessment projects. This may enable organisations to create greater consistency in the approach used by Assessors in recruitment, development, judging of merit/awards, employee appraisals, and the like.

The organisational sponsor noted, "this is excellent work, from a range of perspectives." Because the project findings were so practical and accessible, they were used to set consistent expectations and support Assessors during multi-rater projects at the participant organisation. This helped to support the organisation's ambition to be at the forefront of innovation in assessment.

Reflections on the Work

Coming from a statistical analytical background, the main learning the Researcher took away from the project was the validity and impact of conducting qualitative research in organisations where context calls for it. Deeply investigating individual experiences of events can be as informative as studying large populations, albeit in different ways.

Acknowledgements

Matthew Atkinson

Chris Dewberry

Analysing Executive Interaction

Overview

In this case study Business Psychology Practitioners worked with the Executive Team of a UK charity who felt they were struggling. Besides a team coaching process, they felt that they could do more. The Chief Executive Officer (CEO) wanted to effectively understand and manage his own and his team's performance at an important time of transformation.

The Practitioners applied a rich mix of Business Psychology tools to deliver meaningful insights the Executive Team could act upon. This process enabled difficult conversations to take place by providing a structure, process and common language.

Challenge

This UK charity organization was in a challenging position: what they had been doing was no longer working; they had to make changes to improve their finances and grow.

They had started working on a major transformation initiative to address these challenges, but it was creating considerable tension in the Executive Team. Unaddressed difficult working relationships and uncertainty over succession planning seemed to be compounding the situation. All this resulted in a senior team who did not appear to be pulling together effectively, at a time when they needed to start driving a real change agenda.

The CEO recognised the need for change, observing that team interaction 'felt like a dinner party' most of the time, because tough conversations simply did not happen. And yet he had not discerned his role in creating this situation, for example when he closed some conversations prematurely.

They consulted a Business Psychology Practitioner, who was an experienced Executive Coach and Facilitator, with a brief to help them achieve a break-through. All stakeholders agreed to work together to see if the psychology-based approach could make that happen.

Approach

Research has shown that groups of senior leaders find it difficult to perform as a team (Hackman, 1990). Feedback is seldom offered at a senior level (Kaplan, 2011), although receiving it can significantly enhance performance (Kluger & DeNisi, 1996), particularly when it is specific and objective (Edmunds, et al., 2010).

The Consultant's experience indicated that senior teams want data and designed a solution to provide that in abundance. She elected to use a mix of Behavioural Analysis, 270° and 180° feedback based on predefined behaviours, a semi-structured interview, the Neuroticism, Extraversion, Openness Personality Inventory (NEO PI), as well as group and one-to-one feedback. This rich mix picked up on behavioural and personality themes, looking at them from different angles. This would provide the Executive Team with insight to reflect, and act, upon.

Behavioural Analysis

Behaviour Analysis is a form of interaction analysis used to observe behaviours (referred to as 'utterances') of individuals in a group and the overall behaviour of the group itself. It helps to identify behaviour patterns and has been indicated to be one of the most objective methods of observation analysis (Rae, 2002).

McCredie (McCredie, 1991) described a selection of behaviours determining discrete observation categories used in Behavioural Analysis. The categories used included: Proposing; Building; Supporting; Testing Understanding; Summarising; Seeking Information; Giving Information; Bringing In; Shutting Out; Disagreeing; and Defending/Attacking.

The Practitioners also added categories based on their experience:

- Signposting: offers structure to information given
- Requesting Action and Confirming Request: provides insight into relationships and interdependencies within the team
- Seeking Opinions, Seeking Feelings, Giving Opinions and Giving Feelings: offer granularity about the specific type of information given. These are important when managing complexity and change

- Social Interaction: indicates relationship beyond transactional and discussion processes
- Noise: influences the efficiency of the meeting
- Positive Fillers: reveal mutual involvement and encouragement

In total there were 21 (excluding Defending/Attacking) individual behaviours to categorize. In addition, conversation flow was notated by the Consultants in real time, to see where relationships, power and influence lay.

In order to reliably categorise behaviours, each meeting was observed, video-recorded and transcribed. Once transcribed, all verbal utterance made by the attendees were both categorised and timed to quantify types of behaviours and timings by individual and by group. After the meeting, attendees filled out a 'perceived meeting effectiveness' questionnaire. This questionnaire was based on items described by Jung & Sosik (Jung & Sosik, 2002). Perceived meeting effectiveness was then compared to behaviours and timings established by the Behavioural Analysis.

Aligned Analysis

In addition to Behavioural Analysis, leadership behaviour data were collected through:

- semi-structured interviews
- 180°/270° assessments
- NEO-PI

Findings were collated and described in written reports, produced at an individual and team level. The Executive Team report was shared with the CEO and the individual reports were shared with each team member.

The team report included the Consultants' findings regarding behaviours shown during Executive Team meetings. (See graph.)

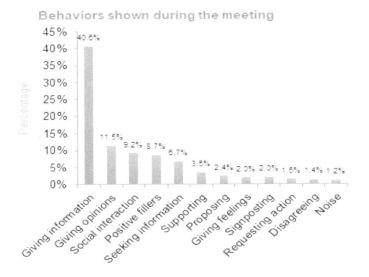

Behaviors shown during the meeting

- The top four behaviours comprised 70% of the overall behaviours analysed: these were Giving Information, Giving Opinion, Social Interaction and Positive Fillers

- Giving Information and Giving Opinions made up 52.1% of overall behaviours: together they indicated sharing but not action, problem solving, or collaboration. Given that there were pre-reads for many of the topics, the Practitioners observed that there appeared to be duplication between what had been read and what was then stated

- Social Interaction and Positive Fillers ('great,' 'good') comprised 17.9% of the overall behaviours, which the Consultants believed to indicate high levels of connectedness and trust, as well as a readiness for open conversation and potential willingness to get to the next level; the team needed a little push towards this, given how little disagreeing there was during this meeting. However, the minimal disagreement observed also indicated to them that the team needed some more encouragement in this area

- Behaviours classified as either Seeking Feelings, Seeking Opinions, Summarizing, Building, Confirming Request, Testing Understanding, Shutting Out, or Seeking Ideas accounted for ≤1% of the interactions

On review, Executive Team meetings did not appear to be an effective use of senior leadership time, and that this was true for the majority of the team's meetings. This insight presented an opportunity for positive change.

Further, when individuals received their feedback report, each was encouraged to review it by analysing which data was shocking, surprising, challenging or a confirmation of their existing perspective. They were then invited to share this with each other as a group, and to decide what to do as a team. This was facilitated by two Coaches; one to lead the session and the other to observe the process and individuals.

Outcome

Insight Delivered

The Charity's CEO observed, "It is immensely interesting to hear your reflections on the way that we work from the perspective of someone who had observed a lot of other senior teams over the years, and it is really making me think. I was frankly astonished by how much you picked up during our Executive Team meetings and the subsequent analysis."

Practical Outcomes

- The Executive Team realised they would need to change the purpose and content of their meetings if they were to drive transformation. Writing better briefing papers and reading them in advance needed to become the order of the day, to prevent everyone simply repeating information and wasting time
- The CEO became aware that transactional business did not add value or momentum. The efficient use of an agenda was unimportant if the meeting content failed to drive the organization forward and match the context
- The COO, who was ear-marked for the CEO role, was removed from the succession plan, as there was clear videoed evidence of undermining and blocking; this was reinforced by the 270° feedback. He also failed to engage collaboratively with the women in the meeting (for example, see conversation tracker visual below, where there were no comments between Exec D and Exec H)

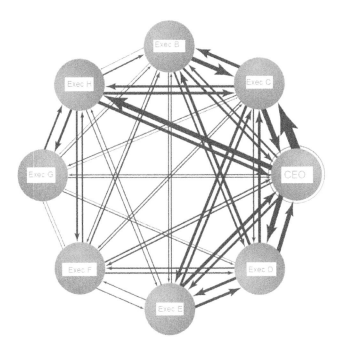

- Intriguingly, the person who spoke most throughout the meeting thought the meeting was least effective
- The CFO improved his contributions to the meetings and his preparation, once he saw how little he was adding to those meetings, and understood others' perceptions of that
- The team started to focus on quality of conversation, not quantity of subjects covered in their meetings
- Individuals started to sit in different places to change the dynamics of the room. They started to evaluate all their meetings as part of a regular feedback processes
- A regular team Coach used the individual reports in one-to-one work
- The team committed to repeating the process the following year to reassess themselves

Acknowledgements

Jessica Pryce-Jones, Joint CEO, iOpener Institute for People and Performance

Susan Pratley

Sanne Dijkema

From Crisis to Culture Health

Overview

RSA is an insurance company that has been operating for over 300 years, employing thousands of people globally with enviable levels of employee engagement. A few years ago, however, they experienced a significant shock when "inappropriate collaboration" in their Irish business made headlines.

Trust was broken inside and outside the organisation and the Chairman made a personal commitment that that would never happen again. In response a custom Culture Health Assessment, based around a Culture Health Index, was created to surface early warning signs of cultural risk.

Challenge

RSA have won awards for having world-class employee engagement levels in many countries; they have ranked as the highest insurer in the Superbrands® index in the past, and have always taken pride in genuinely 'being there for their customers when they need us most.'

So, when issues were uncovered within the Irish business that led to a £200m write down, three profits warnings, and ultimately the resignation of their Group CEO, shock rippled through the company. The independent investigation into these issues uncovered "inappropriate collaboration between a small number of senior management."

Trust and confidence across the business was broken and Chairman Martin Scicluna made a personal commitment to the employees, customers and shareholders that this type of thing would never happen again in RSA.

Internal and external investigations led to much reflection on what could have been done at an individual, team and organisational level to have spotted and managed the potential warning signs.

The project brief was broad:

- to learn the lessons from 'the Ireland case'
- to implement something that would help RSA "prevent another Ireland"

Despite the broad brief, the team assigned felt that there wasn't appetite for a large culture change programme with workshops to define the "as is" culture and "to be" culture. Many issues needed to be addressed quickly and effectively, and several projects were kicked off which would result in system, procedural and policy changes. These, in turn, would have a direct or indirect impact on the culture. They needed something that would work alongside and complement other changes taking place across the business; as well as business as usual processes and practices that impact culture, such as leadership, performance management, communications, company values, and more.

Another challenge was that RSA, as a highly technical and regulated financial services organisation, had great emphasis on numbers, data and risk management controls. Whilst there was increased interest in culture, post the Ireland case, the team found that focusing on culture, behaviours and feelings was not generally within people's comfort zone.

Approach

Applying Science

Internal and external research was conducted to understand the root causes of historical high-profile failures within RSA. The team designing the solution wanted to learn lessons from external high-profile organisational failures, exploring what other companies and consultancies were doing, as well as existing solutions in the market.

Whilst their research highlighted common behavioural drivers and root causes of organisational risk, they found that there was little in the form of practical solutions in the market that would meet their needs. Having established that there was no ideal method available, to predict and prevent cultural or behavioural risk in their organisation, they created an in-house solution.

Tool Design

To manage the scope and unintended consequences of the project, they created design principles. For example, the solution should:

- be effective to administer and easy to report on
- comprise of multiple methods and observers to increase reliability

- operate from principles of trust and safety, not seeking to "trip people up" or create a "police state"
- not link to performance ratings

The solution design team worked closely with senior Risk and Audit Leaders to create a solution that was practical and beneficial to an audience beyond HR.

The lessons from RSA Ireland highlighted that often trust, common sense, diligence and honest conversations went a long way. With this insight, a quarterly Culture Health Assessment approach was designed. This involved semi-structured discussions between HR leaders on the cultural health of each business area. The output of these quarterly reviews included: red flags (concerns), green flags (strengths), and mitigating actions to address concerns.

Twice yearly these reviews were extended to Regional Chief Risk Officers and Regional Chief Auditors to bring in different perspectives and challenges. The value of these quarterly reviews lay in:

- providing an opportunity for core individuals to step back from day-to-day business operations, and reflect on potential organisational risks
- comparing and/or joining-up different experiences
- ensuring action and accountability at every level to address concerns

To facilitate structure and objectivity in the reviews they also designed a 'Culture Health Index.' This included quantitative and qualitative positive and negative indicators, based on behavioural drivers of culture. The index was not a diagnostic or algorithm to predict the type and likelihood of risk, but served more as a guide, providing language to name the behaviours or patterns that people may intuitively recognise, but find hard to describe or challenge.

The design of the index drew on psychological literature which addressed topics such as ethical leadership, Jungian types, psychopaths at work, group think, cognitive biases, and others.

Pilot

A three-month pilot was conducted to test reliability and utility of the tools and secure buy-in. This included:

- Creating training for the global HR community to help develop a deeper understanding of the new process, potential challenges, and the psychology around "why good people do bad things"
- Various country visits to conduct culture audits
- One cycle of Culture Health Assessments

After this was successful, the new tools were implemented.

Outcome

Face Validity

The feedback received on the look and feel of the new tools was unanimously positive, with very few changes required after the pilot.

Specific comments from HR leaders included:

- "The Index gives colleagues a language to name behaviours that they might experience or intuitively recognise"
- The Index "captures the many aspects of culture"
- "This provides a healthy set of questions for a Human Resources leader to be asking themselves about individuals and teams, as part of business as usual"

Positive feedback from external bodies was received, such as The Prudential Regulation Authority (PRA) and consultancies Towers Watson and PwC.

"The work that RSA is doing on cultural risk in particular will ensure that enhancements to the overall control environment will be sustainable and underpinned by behaviour." – *PwC interim s.166 report to PRA*

Overall Utility and Business Benefits

Some of the broader benefits experienced included:

- Greater consistency across the global HR community in how they assess culture and comfort levels around the role they play to challenge culture and behaviours
- Capturing good practice across RSA and examples of strong positive cultures which they can learn from and share
- Facilitating a culture in which individuals would feel comfortable to speak up and challenge inappropriate behaviour. Examples of this increased comfort were seen from the first conversations at senior

levels in which people discussed topics they might not otherwise have had courage, or perceived permission, to address

- Clear accountability for action; this process assigned accountability for action at different levels and provided clear escalation steps to ensure emerging risks were dealt with in a robust and consistent manner. When a quarterly review resulted in a 'red flag' for any particular individual, these were shared with the individual in a transparent and constructive way

- Reassurance to the Group Board and Group Executive that they have greater resilience around cultural risk

Stakeholder Comments

"I believe that the Cultural Health Index will be invaluable in helping us to monitor and assess the organisation's culture. The way it was developed, with extensive internal consultation taking the time to understand the many aspects of culture and requirements, was excellent." – *Group Chief Auditor*

"This work was born out of necessity following specific and significant issues in our Irish business that had gone undetected for a number of years. However, it's impact has been more global and positive than we could have hoped." - *Group HR Director*

Acknowledgements

Kam Somal, Group Head of Organisational Development, RSA Group

Jeremy Phillips-Powell, Group Talent & Organisational Effectiveness Director, RSA Group

Ranking Potential

Overview

The Rank Group PLC (Rank) is the UK's largest multi-channel casino operator, operating in a market with constantly changing consumer spending habits presenting unpredictable opportunities and challenges.

They approached Business Psychologists to help them implement an objective and robust methodology to assess 'high potential' employees, to create a leadership pipeline for the future. Find out how they addressed the Executive Board's perspective on talent within Rank Group.

Challenge

In the past, Rank had used only ad hoc assessment processes and subjective appraisal reviews to evaluate their talent. It required Board level buy-in to invest in the talent within the organisation, to develop their employees to have diverse skillsets, enabling agility in response to change.

Changing the Executive Board's viewpoint on talent and their employees' potential was therefore a crucial step in changing the learning and development culture within Rank Group. They approached Business Psychologists at BeTalent to assist them.

They set four main objectives for the work to be done:

– Create a broader understanding of talent across Rank, using a technology-based solution

– Standardise assessment across the Group, to encourage lateral movement and connect siloed teams

– Educate the Executive Board about the difference between talent and potential

– Identify and facilitate career paths within the Rank workforce, encouraging individuals to champion their own careers

In one survey, 84% of talent management professionals stated that the demand for 'high potential' (HiPo) employees has increased over the last five years due to growth and competitive pressure. Research has shown that HiPo behaviours are displayed in individuals who significantly and consistently outperform their peers in a variety of settings and circumstances (Ready, Conger & Hill, 2010). It is estimated that HiPo employees constitute 3-5% of a company's talent. This research informed the approach taken to develop an effective employee development proposition across Rank Group, and to further understand capabilities of employees at all levels.

Approach

Stakeholder Engagement

The Business Psychologists and client partnered to co-create an employee assessment process, beginning with identifying 'What Great Looks Like' within Rank.

They approached the project through a staged approach allowing time to gather feedback from critical stakeholders to ensure that the solution was fit for purpose. Each stage of the project was reviewed by a group of client stakeholders. BeTalent shared ideas about new ways of working through regular conference calls between the two parties, so that risks could be mitigated, and any concerns could be addressed.

Research and Define

The Practitioners undertook an exploration into 'What Great Looks Like" for Rank through conducting critical interviews with key stakeholders at each organisational level being assessed (Individual Contributor, Manager and Leader). They also asked a variety of employees to complete an online mobile-enabled card sort activity, asking them their views on macro and micro challenges facing Rank. They were then asked to identify the critical behaviours needed for Rank to overcome these challenges. This approach stemmed from BeTalent's model of potential.

Following five years' research BeTalent produced the BEST+ model of potential. Research sources included:

- Caron, D, 2009, It's a VUCA world, CIPS
- Cherniss, Goleman, Emmerling, Cowan & Adler, 1998, Bringing emotional intelligence to the workplace
- Kinsinger & Walch, 2012, Living and leading in a VUCA world
- MacRae & Furnham, 2014, High potential: How to spot, manage and develop talented people at work

- McKinsey, 2011
- Ready, Conger & Hill, 2010, Are you a high potential, Harvard Business Review
- Robertson & Smith, 2001, Personnel selection
- Scott & Reynolds, 2010, Handbook of workplace assessment (Vol. 32)
- Sullivan, 2012, VUCA: the new normal for talent management and workforce planning

The BeTalent BEST+ model is made up of:

- Behaviours
- Expertise
- Strengths
- Tenets
- Aspirations
- Engagement
- Emotion
- Social and Learning Agility/Cognitive Intelligence

These dimensions of potential combined to form the BeTalent potential model. From this model they identified the critical requirements for high performance at the three different levels within Rank Group.

Talent Fit Assessment

- Pilot: The team designed and piloted a tailored high-potential assessment tool based on the criteria identified in Stage 1, with 30 individuals, to ensure that the tool was fit for purpose
- Roll Out: They identified a HiPo population through a mix of self-nomination and managers/HR recommendations. These 350 individuals were asked to rate themselves on the identified key criteria using an online assessment tool. Managers and senior/peer stakeholders were invited to contribute, providing a holistic view of the employee's potential.

This assessment was delivered through a mobile-enabled application where employees and their raters completed the assessment. Each individual received an automated feedback report, as well as a coaching session to identify strengths and areas for development to achieve their career goals. And, based on their assessment results, they were then rank ordered.

The top 31 ranked employees from the Talent Fit assessment were invited to an Assessment for Development event to further understand their potential and talent. This was designed to stretch the individuals through different exercises, including:

– Blended structured interview

– Insight emotional intelligence interview

– Case study

– Presentation

– Roleplay

– Cognitive testing

These exercises were selected based on their reliability and validity to predict performance and potential. (For example, Robertson & Smith, 2001 concluded that structured interview in combination with cognitive ability tests were the most predictive of future performance.) HR staff were trained in these best practice methods and used as Assessors to assist Rank in becoming self-sufficient to conduct these assessments in future.

Individual and group performance on these exercises was then analysed to identify individuals demonstrating potential across the business, highlighting common themes across the population. Each individual also received feedback in a personalised development session, to explore their strengths and development areas.

Project Plan

As well as remaining in regular contact with the project team at Rank, BeTalent also actively involved the Executive Board in the project with the aim of changing their views on talent assessment and the learning and development culture in the business. Through a series of presentations, following each phase of the project, BeTalent explored the results and key themes that may have needed to be addressed. This served as an education mechanism to assist the Executive Board in understanding the importance of identifying talent and the role of effective assessment methods in doing so.

Outcome

Following the completion of the assessment events, evaluation of the assessment was conducted to assess the impact of the solution on Rank Group's HR strategy and employee development.

Candidate Feedback

All candidates that undertook the Assessment for Development process were asked to fill out a feedback form containing both qualitative (text response) and quantitative questions (rated strongly agree=4 to strongly disagree=1). The results suggested most of the assessed population found the event useful for their development:

- I found the event useful today: 3.77
- I was able to maintain focus throughout today: 3.40
- The format and context were relevant to Rank: 3.50
- The Assessors were helpful and communicated clearly: 3.90
- I believe the feedback report will help me with my career development: 3.63
- Overall rating: 3.74

The qualitative feedback was used to further improve the assessment event for Cohort 2.

Human Resources Feedback

During an initial impact evaluation interview the Human Resources Director commented:

"Helped to get a clearer and more objective view – helped think about talent. We now have a plan in place and have managed to get the board to think differently about talent…"

"We are talking more about using talent to succession plan, we have ended up in a place that helps shape what we do next, now feels like a more objective view to talent and talent planning" - *David Balls HRD*

These comments show that the project resonated with the Executive Board. Ultimately, the shift in perspective that was observed by the HRD had an impact on the culture of the organisation by changing attitudes towards the way that assessment can be delivered using multiple methods for both recruitment and assessment (i.e. face-to-face and technology). They later began considering implementing similar strategies using the capability research in Stage 1 to recruit external hires.

Acknowledgements

Dr Amanda Potter BSc (Hons) MSc AfBPSs HMABP CPsychol CSci

Section Four:
Assessment for a Greater Good

In this final section we look at assessment interventions applied in broader and more ambitious settings.

First, we see how Business Psychology was applied to support Health Education England's Pharmacist Education and Training Reforms programme, to facilitate a wider change in the profession and the role of pharmacy in healthcare.

Second, we see how a pragmatic Fire Service recognized an opportunity to use science to address concerns raised around their Operational Preparedness. This case shows that learning from tragedy can have a long-term positive impact.

Third we learn from London's Metropolitan Police Service, tackling the opportunities and challenges associated with the diversity of Londoners they service. Their approach to assessing Intercultural Competence has effectively improved Police Constable hiring.

Fourth we learn from Vodafone and the significant investment they have made to support youth employment. Recognising the global tragedy of youth unemployment and its impact on society, they took practical steps to help youths identify job opportunities and learning opportunities that would better equip them to achieve employment.

Penultimately, we look at the high stakes environment of social work, in children's services, and how assessment has been used to truly engage candidates in a relevant and valid assessment experience.

Then we conclude with the National Careers Service (NCS) and investments they have made in the "Skills Health Check" assessment, to potentially meet the needs of the c.40 million people who use their services each year.

Future Pharmacist Selection

Overview

Health Education England (HEE) aims to deliver a responsive pharmacy workforce in the UK, equipped with the skills to deliver a clinical service across all care settings, and adapted to new ways of working. This supports the NHS's plan to make more appropriate use of pharmacy professionals' clinical skills, helping patients get the right care, at the right time, in the right place.

HEE's Pharmacist Education and Training Reforms (PETR) programme sought to facilitate a wider change in the profession and the role of pharmacy in healthcare. It aimed to deliver a responsive pharmacy workforce equipped with the skills to deliver a clinical service across all care settings and adapt to new ways of working.

HEE recognised it was essential for pre-registration pharmacist recruitment and selection to be reliable, valid, acceptable, cost effective and fair, to have a positive impact on education, training and quality in the profession. So, Business Psychologists at Work Psychology Group (WPG) were commissioned to work on the PETR programme. They supported the development of a national recruitment process for all pre-registration trainee pharmacists across hospitals, community pharmacies and general practice. This is their account of the experience.

Challenge

In the UK, Pharmacists started with 'pre-registration,' training which included a pre-registration placement (at least 52 weeks in an approved training site under the supervision of a tutor), followed by a registration assessment.

As part of the HEE PETR programme, a decision was made to standardise recruitment into all HEE funded pre-registration pharmacist training positions. During the pre-registration year, trainees are employed predominantly in either NHS hospitals or community pharmacies in the private sector. Within the NHS, recruitment into pre-registration training posts in England and Wales had previously been managed through the NHS Pre-Registration

Recruitment Scheme. The process of managing applications and making offers was carried out at either a regional or Trust level.

This posed a number of challenges. For example, pre-registration pharmacists applying for one of the HEE funded roles may have to sit multiple assessments against inconsistent criteria. As the facets of personal attributes required for the role were not explicit, these varied by definition or importance dependent on employer or sector of practice. Applications were also staggered, with a variety of timeframes within which job offers had to be accepted, meaning that applicants may have to had to make a decision on accepting a role prior to knowing whether they were successful in other applications. There was thus a clear need to develop standardised, valid and evidence-based methods for recruiting and selecting pharmacist trainees for pre-registration training, that also clearly aligned with the values of the NHS.

Pharmacists played a vital role in helping the NHS shift from acute to integrated care, fulfilling the pressing need to do more for less. So, another theme in the development of a national recruitment process was that the role of pharmacy in the NHS was evolving. The skills Pharmacists needed were therefore shifting; Pharmacists had to increase focus on engaging with patients to support long-term conditions, providing enhanced services and promoting healthier lifestyles.

The work of the Business Psychologists was carried out in this context, with Pharmacists having to work alongside government and regulators to set the agenda for change in policy, and align stakeholders across the spectrum of commissioners, clinicians, pharmacy contractors, and patients. Whilst this project focused on the recruitment process within England and Wales, it had international implications as careers within pharmacy continued to evolve across the globe, impacting healthcare outcomes of the future.

Approach

The project was split into two phases; developing a Professional Attributes Framework (PAF), and the development, implementation and evaluation of a multi-trait, multi-method selection process whereby students apply through one route for all pre-registration pharmacist training positions across England and Wales.

It was important that a robust, evidence-based approach was utilised to provide an accurate and clear attributes framework, but also to support stakeholders in implementing a considerable change programme within the pharmacy education system.

A multi-method role analysis was conducted, consisting of a desk-top review, interviews and focus groups with stakeholders (n=63), consultation during recruitment workshops (n=c.150), and a validation questionnaire asking respondents to rate the importance of the attributes identified (n=867). Overall, c.1,080 individuals participated, providing a wide range of perspectives and facilitating stakeholder engagement.

Through data analysis, nine attributes were identified, each represented by several behavioural descriptors. Questionnaire results indicated all attributes were considered important by stakeholders. This provided justification for the PAF, to be used as the basis for selection criteria and to inform future pre-registration pharmacists selection.

Tool Design

The next stage was to design a multi-trait, multi-method selection process. Adopting this approach to selection, with each attribute being assessed multiple times, enhanced both the validity and reliability of the selection process.

When selecting the methods to employ, a number of factors were considered including ability to assess the attributes identified, evidence of reliability and validity, cost-effectiveness and practicality. On this basis, the methods selected were:

– A Selection Centre (SC)

> The SC allowed multiple measurements of attributes across different exercises whilst also providing the opportunity for applicants to meet with Assessors and respond to open questions

– A Situational Judgement Test (SJT)

> The SJT was selected to accurately assess non-academic attributes in a reliable way. Further, due to the nature of the selection process (i.e. to rank applicants to allocate placement

choices), the SJT had the further benefit of providing a large score range, offering the granularity required for ranking

– A numeracy test

This assessment was included in the recruitment process, with numeracy being an essential skill to ensure therapeutic dosing, safe administration and correct supply of medications. Whilst the numeracy test score was not used to determine the final applicant ranking, an applicant was required to 'pass' this element of the process to be offered a place

SC exercise development interviews were conducted with SMEs (n=9) using critical incident technique; the interviews aimed to elicit situations that pre-registration Pharmacists may face. Once developed, exercises were reviewed to ensure relevance to the target role, fairness, as well as equivalence in terms of the level of difficulty between the versions used across the circuits.

Four SJT item development workshops were held, followed by two review workshops, with Subject Matter Experts (SMEs) who had the appropriate expertise and were close to the pre-registration Pharmacist role. The review workshops aimed to gain input in relation to contextual relevance, realism and fairness of the items developed.

SJT items and SC exercises were piloted across 15 sites within England and Wales, including pre-registration Pharmacy events and six Schools of Pharmacy. During the pilot, 617 participants completed the SJT and 13 faculty members and 26 students completed the SC. Following evaluation, amendments were made where required and the final assessments confirmed.

The SJT contained a total of 52 scenarios, comprised of both ranking and multiple-choice questions. The SC consisted of six short, practical exercises, each measuring two attributes, assessed by two Assessors. The numeracy test consisted of 10 free response questions.

The national recruitment process was implemented following piloting, with ongoing evaluation.

Outcome

The PAF was well received by stakeholders and the pharmacy profession alike. The robust nature of the approach provided assurance in the outputs, meaning that HEE could confidently assert the use of the framework for pre-registration Pharmacy selection.

Findings suggest that the national recruitment scheme was effective and fair, and supported applicants in being allocated a pre-registration Pharmacy post. Overall, the process was received positively by applicants and stakeholders, with the methods utilised being evidence-based, demonstrating good levels of quality and difficulty and able to successfully differentiate between applicants.

The overall fill-rate was 75%; whilst all hospital posts were filled, for some community pharmacies, fewer posts than anticipated filled. HEE committed to action planning as a result of this to ensure the national scheme increases fill-rates in subsequent years.

Interview Panel Members had positive perceptions regarding the relevance and appropriateness of the SC content as part of the pre-registration Pharmacist selection process. Applicants' perceptions of the SC, SJT and numeracy tests were generally positive in relation to the relevance, appropriateness and fairness of the overall selection methods.

Extensive evaluation of the selection process was undertaken to ensure that the processes used were defensible and robust.

- Analysis of results demonstrated the SJT was a reliable tool, able to differentiate sufficiently between applicants. Item level analysis indicated a good level of item quality and difficulty across the items used

- Analysis of SC outcomes showed a close to even distribution across the four circuits, with each able to differentiate amongst applicants. These initial evaluation findings suggested the circuits were comparable; there was therefore no impact on applicant scores depending on circuit completed

- When investigating the relationship between the SJT and the SC a moderate significant correlation was observed, suggesting that whilst there is a degree of shared variance between these two methods (i.e. performance on one measure is linked to the other), both are adding unique variance to the overall selection process

- Across the 10 numeracy paper versions, the internal reliability was generally acceptable ($\alpha=0.56-\alpha=0.73$). Whilst the reliability is lower than desired it was likely that the reliability was affected by the short test length and the variance associated with observed total scores

- Analysis conducted to investigate differences in performance on the SJT and the SC based on demographic group, indicated small significant differences in relation to age (younger applicants performing better) and ethnicity (White applicants performing better). Small significant differences were also observed on the SJT and SC dependent on an applicants' gender (females performing better)

- Moderate to large effect sizes were found between UK and non-UK applicants across all three methods. Whilst these findings were in line with differences observed in other selection processes for similar professions, it was proposed that differences continue to be monitored as part of any future selection

Ongoing review, evaluation and validation was planned to explore the acceptability and long-term impact on education, training and placement quality.

Acknowledgements

Charlotte Flaxman, WPG

Vicki Ashworth, Associate Director, WPG

Gail Fleming, Dean of Pharmacy & Lead for Pre-Registration Pharmacy National Recruitment

Life Saving Assessment

Overview

Few workers deal with life and death situations as much as those in the Fire Service; these are truly high-stakes jobs. This makes the application of Business Psychology, to address behavioural risks and optimise performance, especially valuable here.

The forward-thinking West Midlands Fire Service recognized an opportunity to use science to address concerns raised around their Operational Preparedness.

When optimal preparedness can save lives, focused individual assessment and development can be delivered to optimise success. And in highly specialised jobs, this should be done in highly customised ways.

This case shows that learning from tragedy can have a long-term positive impact.

Challenge

A fire at a vegetable packing plant that took around 24 hours to control claimed the lives of four fire personnel. The Incident Commanders were accused of negligence with claims that tragedy resulted from heuristic-assisted decision-making (or bias). Claims were subsequently dropped but concerns remained.

In another incident, a woman fell down a disused mine shaft and subsequently died. This case raised a new set of questions about responders' knowledge, communication, co-ordination and preparedness.

What could the service learn from these tragedies? And could the threat of prosecutions make personnel more risk-averse in the future? Might that, in turn, impact their effectiveness? The West Midlands Fire Service contracted Business Psychologists to address these concerns.

The Practitioners agreed to measure and evaluate the Service's Operational Preparedness (OP), an essential consideration in their responses to the abovementioned incidents. At the time they found that no model of OP existed, so the first phase of work required them to evaluate OP at an organisational level.

Approach

In their Consultation with the West Midlands Fire Service, the Psychologists found the Service to be incredibly innovative, attempting to revolutionise public and staff safety. This gave them confidence that the application of robust scientific solutions would be respected.

First, the Business Psychologists used job analyses and critical incident techniques to develop a model of OP. The five core elements of OP which emerged were:

– Trust
– Information Gathering
– Incident Learning
– Skills
– Experience

This insight was used to inform an organisation-level Situational Judgement Test (SJT).

Early Findings

Overall, the findings suggested that West Midlands Fire Service were mostly prepared to deal with demanding incidents. But a higher risk group came to light: those with Crew, Watch or Station Commander positions, with 21-25 years' service, appeared more prone to risky heuristic use.

These findings were crucial to demonstrate potential areas for attention in certain types of individuals and raised awareness around the more general need for consideration in decision-making processes. In response, for example, 'talk aloud' exercises were introduced to limit the use of heuristics and to encourage more information gathering.

Going Further

In testament to the perceived value delivered by the Business Psychologists' work, West Midlands Fire Service chose to extend the engagement to facilitate developing a greater level of OP in their teams.

The Service commissioned the development of a measurement tool for individuals in Bronze and Silver Commander roles, that would identify opportunities for further training and development in OP.

Bronze Commanders are Operational Commanders; they directly control an organisation's resources at an incident and will usually be with their staff working at the scene. Silver Commanders manage tactical implementation, following the strategic direction given by Gold (Strategic) Commanders and making that into sets of actions to be completed by Bronze.

Applying Science

In selecting the tool and approach to use, to design and implement a solution for a measuring individuals, a variety of research was reviewed. Factors considered included:

- Situational Judgement Tests (SJTs) can be powerful predictors of job performance, per Weekley & Jones, 1997, and Smith & McDaniel 1998; i.e. how an individual answers a question on an SJT can be predictive of how they would act in a similar real work situation
- The value of measuring actual job knowledge has been demonstrated, per Motowidlo, Borman & Schmit, 1997
- SJTs can be designed to effectively capture diverse behaviours, per Chan & Schmitt, 2002, which was suited to the complex work requirements of fire personnel
- SJTs designed upon robust job analyses yielded stronger correlations to subsequent performance, per meta-analysis by McDaniel, et al., 2001
- The use of a critical incident technique to develop items facilitates a more realistic measure, that would be able to competently differentiate between successful and less successful behaviours, per Koch, et al., 2009.
- Best practice procedures for the development of an SJT were available for reference, per Bledow & Frese, 2009; Livens, Buyse & Sackett, 2009, and Steptoe-Warren, 2010

As a result, an SJT approach was adopted to maximise the outcomes from a measure of Operational Preparedness (OP) and provide development-related feedback for the Fire Service.

Tool Design

In order to develop the SJT to assess OP in Bronze Commanders, the project had many phases, all of which necessitated close collaboration with West Midlands Fire Service and its stakeholders:

- First, days were spent shadowing Fire Fighters on duty to ask questions and gain a sense of the roles and responsibilities of different levels and in different environments
- Second, sessions were held where personnel recalled critical incidents and their actions, which were then sculpted into SJT questions and answers
- Subsequent sessions facilitated the clarification of question content and production of appropriate alternative responses
- Items were piloted by 28 personnel with a Cronbach's alpha greater than 0.6; one item identified as problematic was removed
- Finally, using feedback from the pilot, in collaboration with senior members of the Service, items were refined to ensure accuracy and face validity

The scale then underwent more extensive validation, including experimental trials to explore the realism and consistency of performance on the test under normal test conditions and then under stress or exhaustion, to better understand high-pressure decision-making on duty.

An online administration solution was created by the Practitioners so that all those who completed the tool could automatically receive a personal feedback report. The report was designed for ease of use, including an introduction and description of the five key elements of Operational Preparedness assessed. Then the individual's performance on each facet was described along with recommendations for development strategies and a personal action plan.

Due to the audience for this project, it was essential to ensure a high level of face validity in all materials, which directly referenced the environment and experience of this population.

Project Management

Clear objectives and timelines for each stage of progress were explicitly agreed at the start of the project and were met at every level. Before the work would be considered complete, all requirements were met including:

- Provision of a functional and relevant measurement tool that could provide individual feedback
- Creation of a manual for use of the tool
- Training of managers to facilitate feedback dissemination
- Development of training modules for the five areas of OP to support an individuals' development following tool use
- Reporting on observations from the work, with recommendations at an organisational level

Outcome

The way in which West Midlands Fire Service think and act upon development, especially with OP, has changed significantly. This project facilitated long-term changes towards improved OP awareness, understanding, and measurement.

The tool produced an acceptable internal reliability and was integrated into the continuous professional development programme of all Bronze-level Commanders in West Midlands Fire Service. As a testament to the success of the work, the Service then commissioned an appropriate tool for Silver-level Commanders

In addition, experimental research using body-worn cameras during training events – to create a behavioural framework for incident response – was commissioned to further explore the risks surfaced by the research, for example, the use of heuristics.

Lives Saved

The importance of decision-making, trust, and information gathering for fire personnel indicate that the work done to improve OP in the Service likely had significant positive impact. So, whilst one could not specifically attribute any saved lives to this work, the targeted personnel development delivered likely contributed to better outcomes.

Given that OP was fundamental to the losses at the aforementioned Atherstone Plant and Galston Mine events, West Midlands Fire Service and those working on the project felt confident that the changes in understanding gained, and practical use of OP, significantly reduced the possibility of similar events occurring in the future.

Acknowledgements

Dr Gail Steptoe-Warren, Coventry University

Thomas Evans, Coventry University

Phil Loach, Fire Chief, West Midlands Fire Service

Benjamin Brook, Group Commander and Watch Manager, West Midlands Fire Service

Matthew Wroughton

Dr Christine Grant

Ann Diprose

The many members of West Midlands Fire Service who were involved

Intercultural Policing

Overview

London's Metropolitan Police Service (MPS) addresses an area of 620 square miles and a population of over 9 million people. This area is currently home to over 40 communities where at least 300 languages are spoken and many faiths are practised.

Every day the Police take account of the diversity of Londoners they service, and the needs of their different communities. So, when recruiting Police Constables for the MPS, candidates' individual capacity to deal with diversity needed to be considered.

MPS shared this challenge with the Psychologists at a&dc who came up with an innovative response: a reliable and valid test of Intercultural Competence to be used in the sifting of tens of thousands of candidates for Police Constable recruitment. This case study explains how they did it.

Challenge

The MPS has a commitment to policing through consent, with enhanced engagement, participation and community confidence. Working in one of the most diverse, multi-cultural and populated cities in the world, MPS' Constables need keen awareness of these elements in order to work effectively. In the words of then Deputy Mayor for Policing and Crime, Stephen Greenhalgh: "this new policy is about competence rather than colour."

The MPS worked with a&dc to create a recruitment selection tool that could be used as part of the process for Police Constable recruitment, to assess whether a Candidate has the "confidence, empathy and capability to work, engage and deal with a wide range of different cultures." The tool was to be used as part of the candidate sifting process to put 'cultural competence' at the heart of the recruitment strategy.

Prior to this consultation, the MPS had undertaken significant activities to encourage applicants from all communities within London. However, the Consultants observed that the process had not fully taken account of the need for Police Constables, from any community, to be able to interact with people from communities and backgrounds that were different to their own. For a&dc, the first question to address was whether it was even possible to develop a tool with this objective in mind. The Consultants needed to establish whether a reliable, valid and defensible tool could be created to meet the MPS's objectives, and then, within short timescales, develop and implement this tool for use in the next round of Police Constable recruitment.

Approach

Literature Review

The first step for the Consultants was to undertake a literature review to determine whether there was a credible scientific basis for creating a tool of this type. Related research, tools and concepts were identified and reviewed, including:

- Cultural Intelligence (Ang, Van Dyne & Tan, 2011)
- The Multicultural Personality (Van Der Zee & Van Oudenhoven, 2013)
- Intercultural Competence (Gertsen, 1990)

The literature review identified constructs which had clear parallels with 'intercultural competence' as defined by the MPS, and demonstrated that valid assessment of such constructs was possible.

Defining the Approach

The literature review also established two broad approaches to the assessment of intercultural competence:

- directly assessing experience and knowledge of other cultures; or
- tapping into the underlying motivations, attitudes and preferences that underpin comfort with dealing with people who are culturally (or otherwise) different

It was decided that the latter approach was more relevant to the MPS as it:

- did not assume certain levels of experience working with specific groups, reducing the potential for indirect discrimination
- was less likely to lead to social desirability distortion, as items would be more indirectly assessing the construct, and correct answers would therefore be less conspicuous

Developing the Behavioural Framework

Once the project was launched, initial work was undertaken to identify a set of behaviours detailing what intercultural competence looked like to the MPS, around which the tool would be based. To establish these behaviours, a total of 20 interviews were undertaken with a sample of serving Officers across ranks, from Borough Commanders to Police Constables. The interviews used Critical Incident and Repertory Grid Techniques to elicit this information.

The interview outputs were content analysed and 245 separate behaviours were identified. These were then classified into constructs and a Behavioural Framework was created. The final set of dimensions to be assessed in the tool were:

- Empathy
- Relationship-Building
- Open-Mindedness
- Resilience
- Flexibility
- Orientation towards Learning

Developing Test Content

Items for the initial trial version of the assessment questionnaire were written by drawing upon the supporting literature underpinning the construct and related scales and the behavioural framework. A paired statement approach was taken to minimise the impact of socially desirable responding. Both statements in a pair were positively worded, but with one being a construct-relevant statement and the other a distractor item. Participants were required to select which of the statements in each pair was most like them.

The initial item set was trialled on 296 Police Constables. Supervisor ratings of job performance were also gathered from the trial group, so that the validity of the items could feed into final item selection. A final set of items were selected using item facility (i.e. the mean rating of a given item), item discrimination, and the correlation between the item and job performance ratings. On this basis a final set of 60 items was chosen and a norm group created. These items, with an assessment feedback report, were then implemented using an online assessment platform.

Outcome

The Intercultural Competence Assessment (ICCA) was deployed for use in assessing tens of thousands of candidates.

The ICCA was shown to be significantly predictive of managers' ratings of Police Constables' behaviour, with a correlation of $r = 0.20$, (significant at the $p < .001$ level) found. Although a modest correlation, this is uncorrected for any indirect range restriction or reliability of the supervisor ratings. The Consultants thus feel that this result indicates that higher scores on the ICCA were associated with higher job performance ratings.

Additionally, the Cronbach's alpha for the ICCA is 0.81, demonstrating good internal consistency reliability. Significant correlations were found between the ICCA and other related components of the selection process. A correlation between ICCA and a Behavioural and Values questionnaire was 0.27, with the highest correlation (.35) between the ICCA and the Value of Fairness and Respect, providing construct validity evidence for the questionnaire.

Significant correlations were also found between the ICCA overall score and a Situational Judgement Test, which included scenarios about dealing with people from different communities, also used at the sifting stage, of 0.36.

Acknowledgements

Philippa Riley, Principal Consultant, a&dc

Ali Shalfrooshan, Senior Consultant, a&dc

Ross McGarrigle

Dan Hughes

Mary Mescal

A Gen Z Employment Solution

Overview

Youth unemployment, underemployment and a lack of access to appropriate learning, education and career development opportunities has been a large scale and chronic challenge globally for youths, as well as businesses, education and government.

Vodafone decided to take practical action to help youths identify job opportunities, especially digital jobs, and learning opportunities that would better equip them to achieve employment. They created a "Future Job Finder," enabling individuals to be matched to digital jobs and learning opportunities. Read on to find out how they used Business Psychology to achieve this.

Challenge

Youth unemployment and underemployment remain a global dilemma. A study by YouGov, commissioned by Vodafone, found that an estimated 71 million young people are unemployed worldwide. The study surveyed 6,000 young people between the ages of 18 and 24 in South Africa, the Czech Republic, Egypt, Germany, Greece, India, Ireland, Italy, New Zealand, Spain, Turkey and UK. The survey asked for their views on their future career aspirations and concerns.

Two-thirds of those surveyed said they had received 'insufficient' or 'no' career advice at any point in their education or since leaving school or university. Of those who had received career advice, just 15% said the career advice they had received included future-focused digital jobs, 38% felt the advice they had received was focused purely on traditional non-digital roles, and 22% said the career advice they received was 'out-of-date.'

Vodafone decided to take action to help address these issues. They wanted a tool that would offer guidance for young people on the digital jobs they were suited for, and secondly, provide better access to learning and employment opportunities for young people in the digital world.

The 'future jobs' programme was created with an aim of reaching up to 10 million young people across 18 countries. Vodafone wanted to help hundreds of thousands of young people gain the necessary skills to find work in the digital economy by 2022.

They partnered with Business Psychologists at Aon Assessment Solutions (AAS, formerly cut-e) to deliver a global solution.

Leading with a scientific approach, the team decided to build a tool that would bring career guidance and learning opportunities to an unemployed and underemployed youth population.

Approach

Solution Conceptualisation

Vodafone and AAS began with a theoretical approach. Addressing the question, "How do we empower and inform a young person in the world of digital careers?" they recognised that the answer would lie in creating a solution that could:

- Understand each individual's preferred ways of working
- Discover their areas of interest
- Find out what they can do, based on their cognitive ability
- Provide them with personalised advice based on these insights

Vodafone and AAS decided to build the 'Future Jobs Finder' tool, with validated psychometric measures, to be available on a global scale through a mobile-enabled platform. The tool would be designed to be used by anyone, although aimed at the youth population specifically, providing them with digital career matches.

The 'Future Jobs Finder' would provide insight into careers for the users. As well as having a better idea of which roles they would likely enjoy and be more suited for, users would get the additional benefit of broader self-discovery and personal insight through the provision of written feedback on their key strengths. This information could help them build their curriculum vitae (CV).

Project Management

The project was managed by both companies' project managers and consultants centrally in the United Kingdom. A third-party software (Trello) was introduced to ensure all parties were informed and on-track with project deliverables.

The project was managed mostly through an agile methodology, which allowed the teams to systematically research, design, develop, test and make updates to continuously improve the tool without compromising functionality. This methodology is carried out in three-week sprints: two weeks of development and one week of testing, before implementing changes.

The key project phases were:

- Specifications
- User Interface (UI) and User Experience (UX) design
- Model design – defining the digital jobs model and mapping this to assessments
- System content design
- Language translations
- User Acceptance Testing (UAT)
- Load testing
- Documentation
- Implementation

The tool built met the initial challenges outlined above, and the agile methodology employed allowed for continuous improvement of the tool. Enhancements for Version 2.0 focused on the impact the tool had for users; delivering refinements to the approach to engage a larger audience of users.

Applying Science

Research confirming the positive relationship between cognitive ability and career success (e.g. Judge, et al., 1999) is abundant. Similarly, substantial research supports personal preferences and 'fit' as a key indicator for job satisfaction (e.g. Mount, et al., 2005). So, the Designers concluded that measuring a mix of individuals' behaviours, preferences and aptitudes would offer the best input for offering career advice.

A jobs model was created based on a mix of existing models including:

- The Occupational Information Network (O*NET), a database of occupational characteristics and worker requirements information across the U.S. economy which describes occupations in terms of the knowledge, skills, and abilities required, as well as how the

work is performed in terms of tasks, work activities, and other descriptors
- Other job models and occupational classification systems
- Specific 'digital' jobs from job-boards and non-profit organisations like the Tech Partnership
- Other relevant client jobs Vodafone worked with.

The jobs were mapped to existing AAS psychometric assessments, based on detailed job information. In the case of vocational interests and affinities (VIA), they mapped at a scale construct level and used O*NET's six interest areas' data – i.e. Realistic, Investigative, Artistic, Social, Enterprising, and Conventional (RIASEC) – as an evidence-based sense check of their mapping. They then developed and tested different matching algorithms, using O*NET resources, adapting as appropriate.

Having agreed on an initial matching algorithm they tested the tool with a small internal sample, to ensure users would get differentiation and accuracy. Based on findings, they adapted the algorithm and proceeded to Beta testing, to gather more feedback. As they collected data about the jobs the users saved or removed, they were able to refine weighting in the algorithm to increase the accuracy of job-matching.

The assessments used in the tool were all validated, and consisted of a Vocational Interests and Affinities questionnaire (VIA) and a series of cognitive ability tests:
- Working memory
- Visuospatial ability
- Logical reasoning
- Multitasking

The VIA measures behaviours, interests and dispositions based on:
- Gardner's model of multiple intelligences, first outlined in his 1983 book 'Frames of Mind: The Theory of Multiple Intelligences'
- Holland's (1973, 1985) occupational interest themes—Realistic, Investigative, Artistic, Social, Enterprising, Conventional (RIASEC); and
- the Big Five model of personality

The Job Finder Designers made slight adjustments to one part of the questionnaire to assess interest in digital jobs specifically, and adjusted the response format to be more engaging for the youth audience. These adjustments continued to be evaluated as part of the ongoing monitoring of the tool, although they had shown good consistency in the initial analyses.

Insight Delivered

The combined results contributed to displaying specific job matches to users – with live job opportunities (vacancies within Vodafone) for each of their job matches, in their location of choice – and providing further learning opportunities from online universities and free online courses (e.g. Coursera.org).

Outcome

The project saw significant collaboration among stakeholders and delivery teams, working with an agile methodology and holding frequent face-to-face meetings plus regular stand up calls. Together, they built the 'Future Jobs Finder' tool offering a suite of assessments that helped individuals understand their own strengths and abilities, and which then returned specific digital job recommendations and free learning opportunities. Within the first year, it helped more than 200,000 people globally find their digital job matches, employment opportunities and further learning. The tool offered careers guidance and learning opportunities to youths initially in ten languages (subsequently increased) across 19 countries in Europe, Middle East, Africa and Australia.

User Feedback

The Practitioners felt that the most useful way to evaluate the effectiveness of the tool would be to ask the following questions:

- Do users like it?
- Does it direct people to jobs they are likely to enjoy and be good at?

The evidence for the first question suggests a resounding 'yes': strong completion rates and experience ratings of the solution from users, 5-star ratings within the tool and over 90% of users giving a rating of 3 stars or more; approximately 50% give the tool 5 stars.

Regarding the second of these, the literature provides extensive evidence of the validity of the constructs against various measures of job performance including manager ratings, sales figures, goal achievement, Net Promoter Scores etc. So, there are demonstrable links across many job types of the ability of the constructs measured using the tools to predict a person's 'fit' to a job.

Tool Adoption

The team saw substantial uptake across all markets, with the highest uptake rates seen in Turkey, India and Germany, but there was also significant usage in Albania, Greece, Hungary, Ireland, Italy, Portugal, Romania, Spain, United Kingdom, Egypt, Ghana, New Zealand, and South Africa. Users 16-24 years of age comprised 77% of the user base. Many users had either no work experience (47%) or less than a year of work experience (17%), and 37% had only secondary school education. These numbers demonstrated that the tool was achieving the first aim of providing better access to learning and employment opportunities for young people in the digital world.

Out of the approximately 200,000 people who first received job matches, 74,000 viewed employment and learning opportunities for their job matches, which supports the second aim of providing better access to learning and employment opportunities for young people in the digital world.

Finally, based on the early signs of success with this tool, Vodafone approved funding for a next generation version with greater functionality, more attractive design and the global resources to increase reach through marketing and promotion efforts.

Acknowledgements

Vodafone

Aon Assessment Solutions, formerly cut-e

Sophisticated Simulations

Overview

The stakes are high when working to protect vulnerable children. It is essential to ensure the best teams are in place to meet any challenge. So, it makes sense to apply psychology to assessing and enabling Social Workers and associated child protection specialists.

Here we share the approach used by Doncaster Children's Services Trust, which goes beyond typical assessment. Psychologists developed simulations, using 'virtual reality' and 'breaking the fourth wall,' to truly engage candidates in a relevant and valid assessment experience.

Challenge

Doncaster Children's Services Trust was created to work with multi-disciplinary partners and families to protect vulnerable children. Essential to its operation is the recruitment of relevant specialists and their subsequent professional development.

Reports showed that public confidence in child protection professionals was compromised (Munro, 2010). The Business Psychologists at Sten 10 felt it was crucial that the assessment and development of individuals working to safeguard and protect children met high standards. They reflected: "After a series of child protection failures by the local Council, the Doncaster Children's Services Trust (DCST) was set up in... The first of its kind in the UK, DCST operates as a not-for-profit organisation aiming to significantly raise standards of care for vulnerable children in one of the UK's most challenged areas. It does this by bringing together multi-disciplinary professionals – ranging from newly qualified social workers to advanced practitioners, adoption or disability specialists – in rapid response teams, working both for the Trust and indirectly with partner organisations."

A solution was required that allowed objective assessment of the essential knowledge, skills, and behaviours required to provide outstanding care in high stakes, multi-agency situations. And the findings from the assessment would provide input into a Trust-wide learning and development plan. It was important that this assessment was compassionate and positive, so that it did not diminish the morale and confidence of the team, but acted as a catalyst to build commitment and create a common 'best practice' language to raise standards of care across the borough.

Additionally, the intervention needed to align with and integrate the national Children's Care Professional Capabilities Framework (PCF) and Knowledge and Skills Framework (KSF) to create a nationally consistent set of standards of operation for the Trust.

Approach

Defining Objectives

The Psychologists worked closely with the Trust's Chief Operating Officer, his direct reports and a dedicated Project Manager to develop a solution that was engaging and rigorous, yet also cost effective.

Given the pace of change required (initial delivery was required within six weeks), and the significant challenges the Trust faced, they agreed to:

- make the assessment a learning experience, building self-efficacy and confidence for both participants and the internal Assessors
- use a blend of technology with more traditional forms of assessment to create a contemporary, realistic and safe learning experience, that showed the Trust to be innovating in social worker development

The aims for the intervention would be:

- Create a learning experience
- Clear standards
- Common objective
- Shared experience
- Assessment of whole population on time and on budget
- Using insights collected for the Trust Learning & Development Plan

They also identified a need for three versions of the centre, for (1) frontline staff, (2) managers and (3) senior managers. The content would be aligned with a levelled competency framework to reflect the differences at these levels.

Visionary Interviews

Visionary interviews and a focus group with Advanced Social Work Practitioners highlighted the range of stakeholders involved in family care, the complex family dynamics, and emotional content of the work.

This surfaced a need to embed a shared understanding of the indicators of child neglect and the associated remedies, including:

– Awareness of the elements that define child neglect
– Ability to identify and select salient goals to improve the situation
– Ability to effect change in complex one-to-one situations
– Ability to anticipate and plan future actions

Applying Science

Research shows simulations, with expert observation, are an appropriate way to develop the cognitive and behavioural competencies required to operate in high stakes situations. Furthermore, they develop tacit knowledge, shared mental models, and self-efficacy, all key requirements outlined in the Client brief and visionary interviews. (Cited references included Douglas, Jackson & Duncan, 2002. Sternberg et al., 2000. Costello, 2001. Tompson & Dass, 2000.)

Solution Design

The Consultants worked with the Heads of Service, Service Managers and Team Managers. Together they integrated the existing national Professional Capabilities Framework, and the newly published Knowledge and Skills Framework, into a common competency model for use in the centres and beyond.

They held focus groups using Critical Incident (Flanagan, 1954) and Repertory Grid (Kelly, 1955) interviews, which were used for both competency design and to provide ideas for exercise content.

At the same time, the Practitioners used contacts gained from another social work client, Frontline, to reach out to the Centre for Child Protection (CCP) at the University of Kent. Their specialists in training, research and practice aimed at child protection professionals had developed a range of innovative computer-based learning simulations covering various social work issues. Through consultation the team selected "Rosie 2."

Rosie 2 was a research based 'serious game' simulation built around a girl called Rosie and her family. It simulated a 'walk through' of their home and provided various opportunities for the user to choose 'what they would do next'. This offered an innovative, common introduction to the Centre for all participants and became the foundation upon which all exercises were designed.

'Breaking the fourth wall' is an interesting way to get audiences to connect with characters. When on-screen characters engage with the audience, a particularly engaging connection can be made. Using a serious game to initiate role play exercises allowed the Psychologists to draw participants from the 'virtual reality' simulation into 'real life' exercises, to put their behaviours, skills and knowledge to the test in a way that a computer simulation alone could not.

Thus, a series of Assessment Centre exercises were developed that allowed Rosie 2 'characters' to step 'out of the screen' and into 'real life' role play exercises. During the assessment, for example, frontline staff could have a meeting with Rosie's mother, and manager level participants could have a meeting with a social worker who was struggling with the case.

The characters were played by a team of professional actors that were briefed, by social workers, to understand and accurately reflect the challenges and emotional content of the scenarios.

Additional exercises included writing up case notes and prioritising a complex in-tray. To aid learning, each participant captured their development goals and reflections in a log. Research has shown that the quality of the feedback given to participants enhances motivation and self-efficacy and behavioural change. (Stefano, 2014. Tovey, 1997. Thornton et al., 1995.) So, their learning log observations were blended with a structured feedback process against the new framework, delivered by Trust staff.

Outcome

As an outcome, the Trust had a set of common standards, anchored in the Children's Care PCF and KSF, which enabled individuals and managers to reflect on their own strengths and development areas, as well as to receive feedback and support using a 'common language.'

From a process perspective, close collaboration with the Project Manager ensured the integration of the design and delivery aspects were delivered on time and within budget.

The first Learning Centre was held as a pilot with the Heads of Service who formed the first wave of Assessors and sponsored the initiative. In total, 35 managers were trained as expert Assessors, each supporting two or more Learning Centres. In total, 99% of the target population attended a Learning Centre within the targeted two months.

Learning took place on multiple levels:

- Each participant completed their learning logs and then received feedback in order to help create an individual development plan
- The expert Assessors benefited from objectively reviewing each other's teams against a consistent standard, coming together to coach and challenge one another through the process
- Discussions and observations by managers identified broader operational opportunities for the Trust to empower and enable front-line staff and to realise synergies
- The qualitative and quantitative data was analysed in order to identify Trust-wide strengths and areas for development within and across role types, levels and teams. These insights informed the development of the Trust wide Learning and Development Plan

An unexpected benefit was the quality of insights generated by the actors. Drawing on the depth of research underpinning Rosie 2 and the richness of the character briefs, they were able to create a deep and realistic interpretation of the situation and characters. In doing so they not only produced a highly effective learning environment for the participants, but a unique window for the expert Assessors to understand the impact of participant's actions and behaviour on family members in a way that they do not often get the chance to do in 'real life.'

Overall, the Practitioners reported that client feedback was very positive. The project allowed the Trust to align around a common objective, resulting in more clarity about expectations for staff, increased understanding of the key issues facing frontline social workers and the impact they could have.

Acknowledgements

Ben Williams, Managing Director, Sten10

Prof. David Shemmings, Centre for Child Protection at the University of Kent

Dr. Jane Reeves, Centre for Child Protection at the University of Kent

Mark Gurrey, Interim Chief Operating Officer, DCST

Mark Douglas, Chief Operating Officer, DCST

Vicky Schofield, Head of Service, DCST

Victoria Sykes, Project Manager, VSC Ltd.

Robin Bott, Senior Consultant, Sten10

Emma Rees, Business Psychologist, Sten10

Kicking-Off Careers

Overview

In the UK, the National Careers Service (NCS) provides information, advice and guidance to help individuals make decisions on learning, training and work opportunities. The service offers confidential, helpful and impartial advice, supported by qualified Careers Advisers. Their audience are often unemployed individuals, seeking guidance at vulnerable times in their lives.

The NCS relies on many self-service tools to meet the needs of the c.40 million people who use their services each year. One particular tool, the "Skills Health Check" assessment was aimed at a broad variety of UK users ranging from school leavers to the long-term unemployed. It was intended to be particularly empowering for these individuals, but very few people were benefiting from it. So, the NCS consulted Business Psychologists and digital experience specialists to optimise it.

Challenge

NCS' website is designed to improve the employment prospects of its users who range from school leavers to the long-term unemployed. The website attracts upwards of 40 million hits a year. Approximately 39% of users move from unemployment to employment, and about 68% progress into learning.

NCS had offered a "Skills Health Check" assessment. The aim of the assessment had been to create a transparent journey for users' career planning. The ambition was to support improved social mobility and users' individual economic contribution. But NCS decided it was no longer fit for purpose as only 1.2% of visitors to their site chose to complete it. There were also concerns raised that those who did finish the assessment did not get matched to the best opportunities for them.

NCS approached Business Psychologists for support in modifying the tool. The brief was for the new assessment to:

– Retain scientific robustness
– Be visually appealing with a positive user experience

- Use only appropriate language to suit the audience; simple, clear, and accessible to a wide range of people
- Be inclusive, to fit the broad user demographic (both self-service individuals and career advisers)
- Provide outputs with specific job profiles, options, and actionable, encouraging information to help plan a move into a new career

The touchpoint for the assessment was important in increasing users' confidence, at a vulnerable time in their lives. How users reflected on the relevance and application of the results was as important as the results themselves. To do this, results needed to summarise an individual's preferences and offer broad job family suggestions, relating transparently to the questions people were asked.

Business Psychologists at SHL partnered with Design Consultants at Hippo Digital to comprehensively address this need for NCS. SHL provided psychological expertise, providing scientific robustness to evaluate the quality and success of the assessment. Hippo brought expertise as a design agency specialising in public sector user experience. Together they proposed an approach for NCS which gave both the psychological robustness and best-practice website design required to deliver a best-in-class solution.

Approach

The project commenced with research into the needs and experiences of current users, documenting these as a basis for planning how to address the challenges with the existing tool. This informed their design of a new solution which would combat these challenges.

From this, they planned to create a shorter, more succinct and more accessible careers discovery tool that would allow for exploration, empowering the user to make their own development decisions.

Content Design

After the user needs had been identified, content creation work commenced.

First, Psychologists created a framework of career preference to underpin assessment questions by:

- Referencing existing career preference assessments, like the work of Holland, Schein, Hogan, Schwartz and others

- Conducting thematic analysis, a widely used and flexible qualitative analytic method for identifying, analysing, and reporting themes within data; this allowed them to organise and describe datasets in rich detail, identifying patterns and themes, selecting which were of interest
- Facilitating a group workshop where the existing validated frameworks were used to map to a new framework for the project, resulting in identifying eight overarching traits for all job families

Next, they created succinct and simple questions for the framework. This work was based on psychometric best practice, using Trait Activation theory to elicit a response for each of the eight traits. The situation cue of answering a question would result in the individual expressing preference for that item.

The Psychologists then created technical or functional competence questions, to drill down within a job family (a cluster of related jobs) to individual job profiles. Technical competencies defined the essential skills and knowledge that were required for someone to be effective in their role. They described the know-how, tools and techniques required for a role, and were separate from behavioural criteria.

Once users took the assessment, the final page provided them with their top ranked job profiles and displayed information around expected salary, entry level requirements, descriptions of the job, the work environment and other job profile information.

User Experience

Hippo undertook user testing throughout, to provide feedback and optimise the user interface. For example:

- A progress indicator was initially excluded from early prototypes but was added in after feedback from users expressed frustration at the lack of certainty about how far they had got into the assessment
- Iterations tested and developed the response options, ascertaining how many options it was best to present. After user feedback, four response options and a "this doesn't apply to me" option was deemed to be best
- Colour and wording options were iterated to improve accessibility to a broad range of people. The assessment needed to be accessible to a wide range of diverse people, so research was conducted with respondents who experienced Attention Deficit

Hyperactivity Disorder (ADHD), Multiple Sclerosis (MS), Asperger Syndrome (AS), Dyslexia and visual impairment

Project Management

The Consultants used Agile project management methodology consisting of an eight-week discovery sprint, as well as alpha and beta iteration sprints. SHL and Hippo Digital worked closely with their stakeholders at NCS throughout. They accomplished this through regular project meetings and update sessions to inform NCS of progress. They presented back and sought feedback throughout, as well as producing written reports to articulate key assessment stages demonstrating that they were meeting project goals.

Outcome

Various performance measures were monitored, analysed and reported on, against the originally identified user needs. This was to understand the impact on users gaining insight and acting on it – such as researching jobs, seeking further career conversations, understanding their options for further education or even entering employment.

User Feedback

Analysis of user feedback showed:

- 100% of respondents believed the assessment was straightforward
- 73% of respondents agreed that statements encouraged them think about how they responded
- 65% of respondents agreed that the results included careers they might be suited to
- Only 13.5% of respondents felt the results did not reflect their interests or values

Users provided comments such as:

- "Really like the straightforward approach and the percentage indicator showing how much more to go!"
- "It's also a good way of seeing what other areas of work might suit strengths and preferences as a person... It's really comprehensive, clear, and I think the general public will find it incredibly useful!"

Reliability and Validity

Test-re-test reliability as well as validation against a known and established psychometric assessment (the SHL Occupational Personality Questionnaire (OPQ)) was conducted.

Throughout the project, the team held retrospective meetings to share learnings on approaches, feedback and to evaluate the success of each iteration. The Hippo Digital and SHL teams met face-to-face and also involved senior stakeholders from both their businesses as well as senior stakeholders from the NCS to evaluate and review project outcomes and learnings.

Acknowledgements

Helen Farrell, Senior Consultant, SHL

Nina Muir, Senior Consultant, SHL

Chris Brain, Product Owner, HIPPO Digital

Temoor Malik, Delivery Manager, HIPPO Digital

Colin Bull, Technical Architect, HIPPO Digital

Section Five: The Future of Assessment

A point of view, from the Editor.

The Future of Assessment

I make a case, in the introduction to this book, for increased attention to be paid to Talent Evaluation, or Workforce Measurement. I do not see this as an organisational choice – a 'nice to have,' or 'value add,' initiative – but as essential to sustainable business practice.

Business Psychologists can offer highly validated approaches to measuring Talent within an organisation, by which I mean all members of their workforce. I believe existing approaches will only make up a moderate part of this work in future, however. I believe Business Psychologists will be increasingly working with digital insights, big data, advanced analysis and machine learning to achieve necessary insights.

This is my point of view.

The Necessity of Workforce Insight

Optimising your workforce, to achieve the requisite agility for long-term sustainable success, requires **foresight, insight** and **activation** mechanisms. As the world of work changes, new opportunities emerge for us to increase organisational effectiveness in each of these three areas.

My perspective assumes the reader's acceptance of the need for organisational foresight, i.e. to anticipate how their workforce will need to change over time. And it leaves discussion on activation of workforce potential aside too. It seeks to address, specifically, current and emerging opportunities to gain **actionable insight** into your workforce's performance and potential.

The Challenge

Deploying and continually redeploying an agile workforce effectively requires insight. It is necessary to understand how best to use each individual's effort, whether you're working with tens, hundreds or thousands of people. Only then can an organisation consistently have the right people in the right place at the right time, ready to succeed.

Research demonstrates that individuals' potential to add value within the workforce is founded on a combination of **innate** capacities (what they can naturally manage and will typically chose to do), and **learned** competence (what they have trained in, professional, technical and functional skills they've practiced and experienced). Performance can also be highly context specific, so when people fit the context and/or culture of their organisation they are most likely to engage and deploy their capacities and capabilities effectively and sustainably.

The requirement for meaningful insight into worker performance however demands more than data gathering. It necessitates increasing the depth and breadth of data typically available on individuals within an organisation, as well as advanced analysis of that data to validate it and create actionable insight.

The Demand

To make decisions with insight, at the operating speed of modern organisations, workforce data needs to be self-sourcing, always accurate and automatically up to date. To achieve this, valid assessment and measurement needs to be built-in to day-to-day operations. This is in stark contrast to the current norm however, which is woefully underachieving in this respect. Many organisations use validated assessments of worker ability only during recruitment (at best) and subsequent on-the-job performance measurement is often subjective, inconsistent and/or lacking in detail. In contrast, HR practitioners who use multiple listening methods rated their organizational performance and reputation 24% higher than those who do not.

Workers also have a vested interest in fair and objective assessment. Most appreciate transparency and recognise opportunities for personal progression more readily when meaningful workplace assessments are delivered.

The worker perspective becomes increasingly relevant when one considers that almost three in four organisations report difficulties attracting critical-skill employees, and more than half report difficulties retaining them. Reports have indicated that more than 80% of companies are seriously worried about their leadership pipelines and only 8% have strong programs to build leadership skills in their millennial populations. Retention and engagement remain costly challenges around the world. Many executives surveyed by Boston Consulting Group see critical gaps in their ability to fill senior managerial roles in coming years. And 63% of CEOs say they are concerned about the future availability of key skills at all levels.

The Opportunity for Workforce Insight

Digital data collection, big data storage and business analytics solutions are advanced to a point where they can be truly useful tools for generating insight to apply to workforce optimisation. And yet in most organisations, Facebook knows more about an organisation's workforce than its leaders. It is time to learn from that. (For example, see CNBC article, "How to find out what Facebook knows about you." Or, read more about research summarised, "Facebook has the capacity to read us as well as our most intimate companions," by Erman Misirlisoy, PhD.)

Where Code Goes, Data Flows; Analysis Should Follow

The increased use of technology, by workers and in the workplace, has increased the digital performance records available for analysis. For example, employees are increasingly being empowered with secure social, mobile and cloud solutions, like Box, Slack, Connections and Trello for example. As the workforce is increasingly wired, workers' digital activities leave data trails which often reveal what they have done and how they have done it. Patterns emerge which tell us all about workers individually and collectively, in real time: when they work, with whom, what they work on, how they do it, what they share, how their input is received and the impact they have, potentially as a proxy for quality or value of their contribution. We can see when individuals are most positively engaged and productive, or where there are risks such as silos, disruption or negativity.

When effectively integrated, advanced analytics platforms and machine learning can help make sense of the large volume of qualitative and quantitative data being produced. By analysing more of this data we can achieve workforce insight in real time, adding significantly to existing employee data sources, to inform meaningful workplace decisions. And, being entirely data-based, the risk of bias and subjectivity in decisions can be significantly reduced.

By taking such an evidenced-based approach, we have an opportunity to derive objective insight into worker contribution (and, in time, individual value). This in turn can inform inclusive and meritocratic decision-making; remedying organisational practices which have created a legacy of unequal suboptimal outcomes.

It is also reasonable to suggest addressing this opportunity will increase employee engagement and retention. Research shows, "intention to leave is twice as high among employees who do not receive recognition (51%) compared to those who do (25%)."

Social network analysis (SNA) is the process of investigating social structures through the use of networks and graph theory. More than three decades ago, in 1987, John Scott wrote in his, "Social network analysis, a Handbook," "there has been a considerable growth of interest in the potential which is offered by the relatively new techniques of social network analysis. Unfortunately, this potential has been seen as unachievable for many researchers, who have found it difficult to come to grips with the highly technical and mathematical language in which much discussion of these techniques has been cast." Well, what has changed is that this is not 'relatively new' anymore. But it remains highly technical. So I will avoid an in-depth discussion, which would probably be beyond me anyway. But I'd like to illustrate what is available, to help readers visualise how significant these insights can be.

Consider as a starting point the illustrative sociometric star Scott referenced all those years ago.

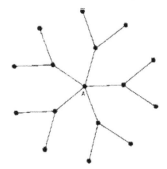

If you were the central character here, you may send a message to five people, each of whom send it to two people, and we can trace how your 'share' reached ten people. In this setting we could describe you as the most influential.

Now put that 'on steroids.' Think back to our chapter on, "Analysing Executive Interaction," and the diagram there which showed interactions between a leadership team. Now imagine that automated for real time production across your entire business to show you dimensions such as:

- Degree: how many people are interacting with each decision-maker or leader in the business
- Closeness: whether the leader interacts as an outlier or in the heart of discussions and decisions
- Between-ness: how interconnected that leader is to the rest of the network (how many individuals get first-hand contact, vs. second, third or tenth-hand messages)
- Influencer score: what volume of output is produced, what reaction it gets, from where, over what period of time

If the image below described a week's interactions in your organisations, which point would likely represent your CEO? And where might you be?

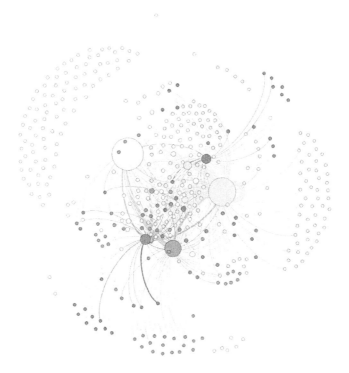

Knowing what this can tell you about individuals' connections and influence, who would you select to advocate for a change programme? Which manager would you say is ready for promotion? Who would you approach for a success story on the value of working across departmental boundaries?

What if you were concerned with diversity and inclusion in your organisation. Imagine how helpful it would be to see whether gender groups (for example) are truly inclusive. Here is an illustrative sociometric for a population of Engineers. Sadly, the lack of integration in the two populations is clear. (But how rewarding it could be to track an inclusivity intervention over time in a population of this sort.)

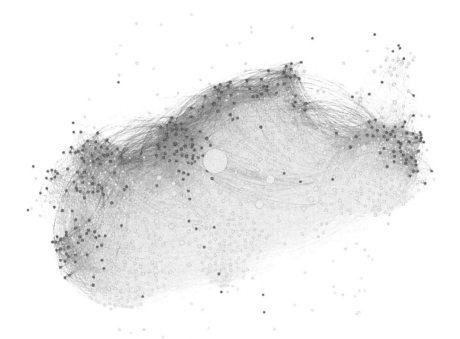

Similar separation could be observed in any other population grouping; differentiating between those positive vs. negative about an initiative for example. Recognising who has influence in each 'camp,' could allow for more focused and effective change management.

Another valuable assessment is to see how business areas behave. There is a legacy that still has many organisations referring to business units as 'Divisions,' unfortunately. How useful it could be to understand the truth of the siloes or integration which exist in practice, in your organisation.

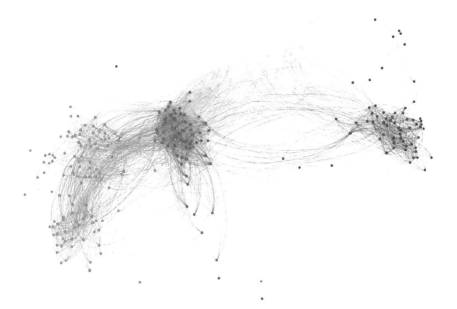

Now, put that all together and bring it back down to the point of this discussion, workforce insight:

> **When we can look at a single individual through all these lenses, and many more, you can start to see if they are connectors, or dividers; if they are influential, or outliers; if they are engaged, or disengaged; if they are heard or ignored; if they are consistent or inconsistent; if they work local or think global; if they give or just receive; if they have particular topics that people consistently approach them about, or no distinguishing feature; and so on.**

All of that from paying attention to information that is already within your organisation's digital infrastructure.

Imagine applying this to measuring the effectiveness of your onboarding programme; how quickly can an individual be integrated within the organisation and informal structures? Perhaps then you will understand how it is that **one organisation predicts attrition in their workforce up to four months before the individual hands in their notice**, because they recognise the patterns of distancing and disengaging often before the individual is even aware of it themselves.

I hope this is helping make my point on the opportunity which exists for significantly increasing your insight into your workforce. Remember here I have only expanded on one type of data you could collect, without intrusion, on your workforce. **Data they automatically produce just by doing their jobs**. Doing analysis that organisations like Facebook have been using for years. I have not discussed the insight that similar content offers into understanding individual's preferences, working styles and sentiment, all of which is already being done for the purposes of digital marketing (think Google Ads). I have not begun to expand on the datapoints beyond communication/networking within your organisation. And I have not proposed using any information that the individual would not already be aware that their organisation has access to, or that, if prompted with opt-in settings like those on Instagram or Twitter, they'd probably share.

Interestingly, I have heard more HR practitioners willing to engage in use of this sort of information for the sake of personalising the worker experience, as that has been trending for a few years thanks to folks like Dan Pink and Jacob Morgan's evangelism on the topic. And yet the extension of the value of doing so for workforce optimisation is seldom addressed at the same time.

Expanding Workforce Insight Now

Accurate, comprehensive, and economical employee assessment is more necessary and more feasible (in terms of efficiency and effectiveness) than in the past. A review of the imperatives for, and enablers of, Talent Evaluation demonstrates this.

Illustrative Imperatives

- Address current and emerging skill gaps
    - Gather insight into current employee skills
    - Assess ability/potential to learn new skills
    - Identify experts/successors for critical roles
- Evaluate resilience of your workforce
    - Measure individual/team agility
    - Address deconstruction of roles, to tasks, for agile resourcing
    - Increase wellbeing, engagement, resilience
- Increase evaluation efficiency and effectiveness
    - Mine data from untapped sources
    - Maintain data with real-time observation
    - Integrate data for increased validation

- Well established valid assessment principles
  - Psychometric practice offers robust standards
  - Digital working captures wider range of data
  - Scientific principles ensure rigour in new tools/approaches
- New data collection methodologies
  - Unstructured data mining tools
  - Non-intrusive observation technology
  - Economical real-time/ongoing data collection
- Automated analysis of integrated data
  - Big data integration solutions to manage data
  - Employee-centric tools for voluntary input
  - Cognitive systems advance practical insights

As these imperatives demonstrate, there is a clear need for embracing new practices to achieve Workforce Insight. Research in the past has suggested as many as 48% of organisations anticipate a skill challenges due to digital transformation. More recently research suggests that employee optimisation in uncertain times will be a product of not only technical ability and practical equipment, but also innate curiosity, autonomy, purpose and embeddedness. Resilience and thriving are workforce aspirations, now more than ever.

These enablers demonstrate that there are new tools available for use to address organisations' needs for effective Talent Evaluation. Cognitive systems offer significant power to increase insight. Research has indicated 50% of HR Executives recognize that cognitive computing has the power to transform key dimensions of HR while 54% believe that cognitive computing will affect key roles in the HR organization.

Business Psychologists understand these concepts, with varying degrees of maturity, and can support evaluation of these characteristics. For pay-off, measurement precision is essential; hence my proposal that organisations work with them to ensure data integrity and defensibility of informed actions taken.

Resources for Expanding Insight

Traditional assessment tools continue to deliver strong results. They create a great basis for Talent Evaluation but can be validated and enhanced by taking a broader view, from multiple perspectives, of employee performance. The broader view may be informed for example by social listening. Consider: research has illustrated measures of personality made by computers on the basis of social behaviour analytics (e.g. activity on Facebook) may be more accurate than colleague, friend or family ratings (with 'work colleague' ratings being least accurate).

Alternative Data Sources for Consideration

Various sources of data may be considered, as illustrated below. Each organisation may find different sources more or less viable, relevant or valid. Overall, however, taking advantage of systems that enable mining of public information, analysing internal information (especially high volume, unstructured data) and extracting behavioural insights from digital activities, will be essential to optimising Workforce Insight as a basis for workforce optimisation in future.

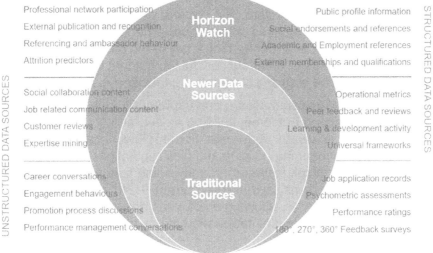

External sources of data are seldom tapped for incumbent (existing employee) assessment, being reserved principally for recruitment purposes (if used at all). Setting aside the arguments 'for' and 'against' the use of this data for the moment, it cannot be denied that a wealth of knowledge about your employees can often be gathered from them. For instance, in a job seeking population, as it relates to their employment, 67% of job seekers have made use of Facebook, 45% use Twitter and 40% use LinkedIn. (Other social platforms, like Instagram, are also gaining ground in employment related activities.) Whilst it is noted that there is variability in the use of these platforms between various income, education and other demographic groups, they remain a potential source of useful insight.

It must also be noted that one would need to use appropriate technology to capitalise on many emerging opportunities for increased data collection. Machine learning (or artificial intelligence) will be essential for this aspect of Workforce Insight collection to be viable. That is, systems which:

- Understand: these systems can receive and process unstructured information in ways similar to humans. They understand language patterns and sensory inputs, including text, pictures and auditory cues. For example, a cognitive system can quickly examine thousands of hours of HR service centre recordings to identify key words and patterns based on frequency, tone and sentiment.

- Reason: these systems grasp underlying concepts, form hypotheses, and infer and extract ideas. They rapidly synthesize information to produce relevant and meaningful responses. Consider the case of a manager who is looking to fill an internal role: A cognitive system could look at various data sources, including a candidate's professional experience and previous performance, and then further analyse the candidate against the characteristics of other successful job holders to determine if he or she would be a strong fit for the organization.

- Learn: these systems learn and improve through every data point, interaction and outcome, building a deep and broad knowledge base that is always up-to-date. In the HR world, with a constant stream of changing policies and new regulations, this capability becomes critical. Rather than addressing a static set of rules, cognitive systems read, tag and organize HR content from a variety of sources, allowing employees access to the most accurate and relevant information at any given time.

Beyond Business Psychology

The Business Case

Investment in any additional assessment requires a business case, typically including plans for a demonstrable return on investment. In this area I suggest pilot programmes be planned and promoted on the basis of what workforce insight leaders have already achieved.

There will always be new case studies shared online, so it is worth searching to find the latest and greatest. I follow David Green for this purpose: @david_green_uk on Twitter, linkedin.com/in/davidrgreen and website davidrgreen.com. He shares a summary of the best talent analytics articles each month with references to new and improved approaches that can inspire, inform and practically help the reader.

Role of Human Resources Teams

HR has a primary role to play in developing the talent evaluation data collection mechanisms and analytics methodology in organisations. Relatedly, policies on data collection, use and application of findings need to be defined. Business stakeholders must be engaged to provide relevant 'triangulation' data – to show context so that business value is demonstrable. This in turn creates basis for actionable insight!

Are you ready to respond to expand your talent evaluation strategy?

Employers interested in investing in an advanced talent evaluation strategy may find it useful to consider:

- What diversity is there in the existing talent evaluation strategy, in terms of assessment type, timing and application?
- What validation mechanisms are used to ensure that what is measured, matters?
- Is scientific method applied when defining talent requirements? Is there clarity across various job families on what constitutes a successful performance, what differentiates top performers and how roles may change in future?
- Are there currently any perceived skills gaps in your organisation? How do you identify and take action on emerging workforce skill requirements?
- What learning-needs-analysis is built-in to the learning functions' strategy, and what employee assessment is that based upon? How is the learning transfer measured in your organisation, and how is that reflected in employee evaluations?
- What incentives exist or could be created to motivate employees to engage with advanced measurement mechanisms?
- What data/privacy policies are in place to protect your employees' interests as greater insight into their performance and contribution becomes available?

Making a Start

The point of view presented here, on increasing Workforce Insight, is intentionally provocative, intended to present an early view of the 'art of the possible' in our working future. And, whilst all of these 'listening' solutions already exist, few are in use to optimal levels and I am not aware of any organisation cohesively mining talent insights in this way (although I've seen some making a great start). So, I thank you for considering this topic and hopefully entering the debate on what is next in the field of 'Assessment.' @clodaghinlondon

References

Sources for statistics quoted in this chapter.

- Bersin, by Deloitte, from https://www2.deloitte.com/us/en/pages/human-capital/topics/latest-thinking-bersin.html
- The Jobvite "Recruiter Nation Survey" from https://www.jobvite.com/wp-content/uploads/2015/09/jobvite_recruiter_nation_2015.pdf
- PwC's Global CEO Study, multiple years, from https://www.pwc.com/gx/en/ceo-agenda/ceosurvey.html
- Deloitte report: Disrupting the CHRO, from https://www2.deloitte.com/us/en/insights/deloitte-review/issue-14/dr14-disrupting-the-chro.html
- CGMA Report: Talent Pipeline Draining Growth: Connecting Human Capital to the Growth Agenda from: http://www.cgma.org/resources/reports/pages/talent-pipeline-draining-growth.aspx
- Paper: "Computer-based personality judgments are more accurate than those made by humans," by Wu Youyoua, Michal Kosinskib and David Stillwella, from https://www.ncbi.nlm.nih.gov/pmc/articles/PMC4313801/
- IBM Institute for Business Value reports:
  - Facing the storm - Navigating the global skills crisis, from https://www.ibm.com/downloads/cas/LBMPLMLJ
  - Extending Expertise: How cognitive computing is transforming HR and the employee experience, from https://www.ibm.com/downloads/cas/QVPR1K7D
  - Performance reviews prevalent but not popular: Research insights into the current state of performance evaluation, from https://www.ibm.com/downloads/cas/XWM4JYMK

- How next-gen computing changes the way we live and work, from https://www.ibm.com/downloads/cas/YVPMGWLP
- IBM Smarter Workforce Institute reports
  - Are traditional HR practices keeping your organization average? From http://www.sift-ag.com/wp-content/uploads/dlm_uploads/Are-Traditional-HR-Practices-Keeping-Your-Organization-Average.pdf
  - Amplifying Employee Voice, from https://www.ibm.com/downloads/cas/08NLPNQA
  - How do I recognize thee? Let me count the ways, Research insights into the impact of multi-channel recognition, from https://www.ibm.com/downloads/cas/EXMEYMZ5
  - Should I stay or should I go? Global insights into employees' decisions to leave their jobs, from https://www.ibm.com/downloads/cas/08GZQKL1

Appendix

An Introduction to Assessment

When referring to 'Assessment' in this document we mean measurement of individuals' (on their own or in groups) abilities/capabilities, skills, characteristics/traits, values or preferences (referred to here as 'constructs') against pre-defined definitions or standards for the construct(s). This document refers to the individuals being Assessed as 'Subjects'. Individuals/organisations using/delivering Assessments are referred to as 'Users.'

Assessment applied in two contexts: (1) most commonly to support recruitment activities by establishing the relative suitability of candidates for job roles and predicting success, and also (2) in change and/or development processes, where existing employees are Assessed for benchmarking, learning needs analysis, performance management, development, redeployment, transition, engagement, workforce expansion or workforce reduction. Research indicates that 'best in class' organisations utilise Assessments consistently, at all levels, throughout the talent lifecycle and in making strategic workforce planning decisions.

There are many overlaps in the tools and processes that apply to these two different contexts (applications), so we will provide a list of factors to consider when making decisions about which Assessment(s) to use.

What Makes a 'Good' Assessment?

Organisations typically 'buy' expertise in Assessment to improve the value/outcomes of their Assessment intervention. Assessment specialists deliver value and better outcomes by delivering solutions that are:

- Valid
- Reliable
- Objective
- Standardised
- Fair

These requirements form the basis of making Assessment interventions fit for purpose and defensible.

However, validity is widely acknowledged to be "the most fundamental consideration" in the development of psychometric measures (American Psychological Association). Any Assessment claiming validity or predictive potential should be clear in what it is measuring, and there must be a demonstrable basis for confidence in the measure. Then it should be applied only where the measurement is relevant and justified.

This is however an understatement. With ongoing debate and little consensus on epistemology or ontology, true 'validation' of psychometric measures may not be realistic. And it is far from typical (perhaps not even possible) to see all measures associated with validity evaluated for any one measure (e.g. accuracy, reliability, factor structure, predictive capability, test scoring, test administration, and social consequences). Nevertheless, measurement provides the foundation for all scientific pursuits, so it is essential to continue to work towards appropriate measurement techniques. (Discussed in useful detail in the "Handbook of Psychometric Testing," chapter, "Psychometric Validity: Establishing the Accuracy and Appropriateness of Psychometric Measures," written by David J. Hughes.)

Rather than assume such an in-depth discussion, I present here a far more accessible guide to considerations in psychometric measurement, hopefully to help those at an earlier stage in the journey to understanding Assessment.

As a starting point we note that Assessments deliver better outcomes if they are:

Valid

Assessments are valid if they measure what they are intended to measure. This means they are (1) well-founded and Assess specifically what they are intended to Assess (e.g. using a group exercise to Assess team interaction, not a written exercise) described as 'construct validity' and (2) relevant to the purpose for which they are being used (e.g. Assessing a seamstress' ability to sew, not to speak a foreign language) described as 'content validity'.

Measurement of Assessment validity is highly specialised in the construction of psychometric Assessments, but the same principles apply across all Assessment tools.

Reliable

A reliable measure is one that measures a construct consistently across time, individuals, and situations. The Assessment must produce consistent results and not be significantly influenced by outside factors. This is ensured to some extent by standardisation of tools (see below). Additionally, using simple language, common concepts, avoiding jargon and highly location/community specific content, will contribute to the longevity of the tool. Training Users to use the tool consistently and effectively is also important.

Reliability is necessary for a test to be valid but is not sufficient on its own. Both reliability and validity can be Assessed statistically.

Objective

Assessment design must reduce the potential for interpretation by individual Assessors/markers to the extent possible. With psychometric tests, where answers are either right or wrong, there is no room for Subjectivity in marking and attributing ratings/scores. When individuals are required to draw conclusions based on evidence collected more Subjectively however, Assessment construction must provide as much guidance, specificity and clarity as possible to reduce the impact of personal opinion and human error in assigning ratings/scores. Assessor training is critical to objectivity in most cases.

Standardised

The way in which Assessment tools are used must be consistent over time. To this end, sound Assessment tools dictate explicitly the conditions under which they should be administered, the time they should take, the equipment that should be provided, the instructions which should be read/supplied, any exceptions that may be made. This ensures that all Subjects are on an 'equal footing' which allows for objective comparison and reduces the influences of context or Subjectivity which may otherwise reduce consistency.

Fair

An Assessment is considered fair if it is fit for purpose. For example, it is fair to Assess the typing skills of a candidate for a role where fast and accurate typing and data capture skills will be required constantly. It is unfair to Assess a Subject's presentation design/delivery skills if the role they have an interest in does not require them to use these skills.

Fairness should not be confused with reliability and standardisation. At times, treating Subjects differently may be justified because of their fundamental differences. For example, an Assessment of numeracy for a first-language Chinese person may be unfair if delivered in English, even if all other Subjects (who are first-language English speakers) are being Assessed in English.

Risks

Related to fairness is the matter of security/confidentiality. Materials used, which are intended to be confidential and only revealed to Subjects in a specific time-frame and/or under specific conditions, should be kept confidential to ensure no Subjects are inadvertently advantaged by having more/different access to the Assessment information.

There are other more significant risks associated with creating Assessment tools or processes without engaging an Assessment specialist. Any or all the factors above may not be suitably applied, each raising risks of inappropriate discrimination and/or Adverse Impact, with legal and ethical implications.

Additionally:

- The construct/s to be Assessed may not be suitably defined/recorded, resulting in the 'meaning' of the results of the Assessment being misunderstood and over/under valued.
- Controls for reduction of bias may not be embedded, increasing the Subjectivity of outcomes (i.e. reducing the validity).
- The infrastructure required to realise benefits from the Assessment is unlikely to be well established/reliable.
- The potential for individuals' performance results to be contaminated with accidental/irrelevant constructs is high, further devaluing the Assessment tool/process.

Local/regional legislative requirements associated with Assessment are beyond the remit of this discussion.

Types of Assessment

Assessment tools can be categorised in various ways, by their content, their purpose, their delivery and application. And many Assessment tools will fit multiple categories. There are costs, advantages and disadvantages associated with each of these. For example:

- Content:

  A common Assessment approach is to ask a Subject capability-based questions

- Purpose:

  To elicit evidence of their past behaviour, as past behaviour has been proven to be a somewhat reliable predictor of future performance

- Delivery:

  Capability-based questions can be delivered in an application form or in an interview. An interview can be applied on one occasion, or on multiple occasions, in person or on the phone, by multiple people and/or panels

- Application:

  For example, a recruitment process, a talent/performance management discussion, a talent benchmarking exercise

- Costs:

  Costs are variable, depending on the delivery method chosen. Reviewing text in application forms might be reasonable for small volumes of recruitment candidates but can quickly become a burden for large volumes. Telephone interviews reduce the resource (e.g. rooms, travel) costs associated with an interview. Face-to-face interviews are the most expensive mechanism for delivering capability-based questions but require consideration of resources including time, ability and commitment of Assessment personnel (e.g. line managers required to conduct interviews). Outsourcing of this task is an option but again will attract costs

- Advantages:

Well-designed capability-based questions are highly 'face valid' which means Subjects will see their relevance and value and can learn more about your expectations when being asked/responding to these. Research suggests that capability-based interviews delivered in a standardised way, by qualified and objective Interviewers, can offer a relatively good prediction of future performance

– Disadvantages:

If capability-based questions are used without proper definitions of the capabilities in advance, in an objective and behavioural way, or if Interviewers are insufficiently trained, there is a high risk of the value of the Assessment being lost

Evaluating Your Options

Assessments can also be 'typed' by their construction and value/quality.

Some of these important differentiators/distinctions between types of Assessment are discussed below. These take various forms and warrant consideration.

– Ranging from more **Subjective** to more **Objective**

Ideally Assessment tools should be as objective as possible. Whenever human intervention is required for interpreting Assessment results, there is a risk of Subjectivity (if unchecked) detracting from the accuracy and validity of the Assessment. For this reason, standardised design, rigorous training and accurate recording of Subjects' performance in Assessment activities is essential. These activities go some way to reducing the risks. Alternatively, and for many a preference, is use of objective measures such as psychometric Assessments to remove this risk.

Most often, in high-risk Assessment processes, a combination of Assessments may be used to include both objective and partially Subjective measures.

– Evidence is **Reported** or **Observed**

A construct can be Assessed by creating an environment in which it can be demonstrated, and then observing the Subjects. For example, the construct of 'collaborative behaviour' could be observed if Subjects are given a group task to complete. The opportunity to observe the construct first-hand, by delivery of/Subject's participation in a standardised and robust Assessment exercise, can offer a positive experience to all in terms of reliability/authenticity of evidence collected. Another example would be a psychometric ability or skills test, where a Subject's ability or skill in responding to questions/tasks is observed.

Alternatively, Subjects can be invited to report their behaviour, ability and/or skills to you. The most common formats for this collection of reported evidence are CVs/resumes and interviews. As the evidence collected in this way is Subject to the Subject's own bias, memory and understanding of the construct, it can lack robustness. This can be overcome to a limited extent by standardising the formats for collecting the evidence (e.g. introducing an application form and using structured interview guides).

Again, in high-risk Assessment processes, a combination of observed and reported Assessments may be used.

– Delivery may be **Time-intensive** or relatively **Quick**

The time required to develop, deliver and score an Assessment tool is relevant for both the tester and the Subject. For example, development of a psychometric tool is highly time intensive and can take months or years. Delivery of a psychometric ability test however can take just minutes. Conducting an hour-long interview can cost five or more hours in total when accounting for the Subject's travel time, the Interviewer's preparation and the follow-up analysis of the Assessment results. Introducing a panel interview format can double that time requirement.

There is no 'right' or 'wrong' decision to be made regarding using quick or time intensive Assessment tools; the point is to be aware of the relevance of each Assessment tool and its value in relation to the time it will take for the User and the Subject. Often a mix will be used with quicker Assessments earlier in the process (with higher volumes of Subjects) and time intensive tools being used later in the process (only for highly desirable Subjects).

– Assessments may be **Simple** or **Complex**

There are various ways to rate Assessment tools on the scale of simple to complex. This could be done by sophistication of constructs, scope of the tool or delivery method. Brief notes on each follow.

- **Sophistication**: a construct may be highly complex and require expertise in its Assessment, for example "deductive reasoning ability". How this ability is defined in psychometric terms is highly complex. A User may think they are able to 'see the logic' in others' reasoning but, in truth, Assessing this construct requires an in-depth understanding of general intelligence, isolation of particular characteristics/constructs, correlations to other abilities/constructs, how to purify the Assessment measure to avoid contamination of outcomes and be entirely consistent in the application of these findings. On the other hand, a construct such as "typing ability" might simply be defined in simple terms of style, speed and accuracy.

- **Scope**: a tool might be designed for a single purpose/audience/application, or for many/a variety. The design requirements will be increasingly demanding. For example, a group exercise may be designed for the Assessment of Subjects in a team at a particular time who are all working in similar roles with similar job demands. On the other hand, a group exercise may be designed to Assess Subjects of varying ages, cultures and levels of experience, interested in working in a variety of roles/business areas. In the first case, use of a highly specialist topic and role specific constructs would be in order. In the latter, use of generic/general interest topics with layers of complexity that challenge different Subjects to different degrees, allowing them to show their relative strength, would be required. And the Assessment constructs used would need to be more generalised.

- **Delivery**: some tools can be delivered online, via the internet, others over the phone or only face-to-face. Some require specific conditions to be present (such as room layout, role play actors, multiple Assessors, etc.) which are more complicated and demanding for the User to facilitate. The collection of evidence can also be increasingly complex. For example: online tools often produce automated results/reports instantaneously, but in-person Assessments often require Assessor training and preparation, administration and Assessment guides, marking instructions and facilitated decision making based on multiple point of view.

– Bespoke or Off-the-Shelf

There are a wide variety of Assessment tools available 'off-the-shelf', which you can buy outright, in packs, units or with a licensing fee, and which can meet most Assessment needs. This is usually the most cost-effective approach to sourcing

Assessment tools, often even more economical than having internal specialists create tools.

Examples of tools typically available 'off-the-shelf', for delivery online and/or paper-based:

- Skills tests
- Ability tests
- Aptitude tests
- Personality inventories (including leadership profilers, motivational profilers, specialist (e.g. sales) profilers, culture fit, 'inclination to engagement' measures and strengths inventories (often associated with coaching and development guides)
- Situational judgement tests
- Case studies
- In-tray exercises (used in Assessing planning, organising, prioritising and similar abilities)
- Role-play exercises (e.g. with sales, customer service or performance coaching scenarios)
- Fact-find exercises (e.g. analysis exercises with commercial, strategic and/or problem-solving elements)
- Presentation exercises
- Group discussion/task exercises
- 360-degree feedback surveys

Purchasing off-the-shelf materials from a reputable Assessment publisher can offer a level of comfort with the validity and value that the tool offers.

There are a number of reasons that Users elect to use bespoke Assessment tools, in all, part or some of their Assessment processes. This typically attracts a higher cost to the User, but delivers the advantages associated with owning unique tools:

- Users can brand the tools and embed their identity in the construction (e.g. reflecting their brand, values and employer value proposition)
- Subjects will not have had access to the tools or have been asked to undertake them previously
- The User's existing (bespoke) competence, capability or technical/functional skills frameworks can be used as a basis for Assessment

- Highly relevant Assessment content can be embedded, reflecting directly the challenges and opportunities associated with specific organisations, teams and jobs; this typically adds to the face validity of the tool and can offer Subjects the advantage of a 'realistic job preview' which can support them in Assessing whether they're a good fit for the organisation, team or job

There are of course many other ways of evaluating and categorising Assessment tools, processes and approaches. We will not consider them all in-depth here, but it is advisable to get advice from a Business Psychologist/Assessment Specialist if you would like insight into various tools' training requirement/s, accessibility and alternative delivery methods.

Bear in mind that many risks to Assessment can be mitigated by avoiding reliance on any single intervention. Avoid over-complicating your Assessment processes however, by not introducing tools beyond those that are relevant and directly add value.

Examples of Commonly Used Assessment Tools

Many options of Assessment tools have already been mentioned. This section provides basic information on the nature and typical application/s of each. This list is not exhaustive but extensive enough to be of use.

These descriptions do not provide the full range of options associated with each tool, e.g. online vs. offline administration, customisation required or recommended, costs, advantages, disadvantages, associated innovations, etc. Advice should be sought from an Assessment specialist if you require further detail.

- Standardised application **forms**:

    Most organisations will invite candidates to submit CVs or resumes, with cover letters perhaps, when applying for a role. Screening applications can be inconsistent as it relies on candidates to supply all the relevant information, without knowing exactly what information you require or the criteria you will use to Assess their application. For example a candidate may not mention 'team leader' experience which they have, as they don't see it as relevant to a non-team leader role; that's not to say they don't have it, but you may exclude them as it is not recorded in the CV/resume whilst it is recorded on others'. This inconsistency can be overcome by defining for candidates what content should be included in applications. This might include requiring candidates to answer specific questions (multiple-choice or text-based) instead of, or in addition to, providing a CV/resume.

In either case, best practice indicates that the criteria that will be used in screening applications should be defined in advance, taking account of practical role requirements (skills and experience) and distinguishing between those that are immediately necessary as opposed to those that are desirable.

– **Skills** tests (also known as attainment tests):

Assess acquired/current level of knowledge or skills (e.g. driving, typing and programming in Java) usually online or on paper with a percentage correct/accuracy score, typically associated to a relevant level (e.g. basic, intermediate or advanced).

– **Ability** tests:

Assessment of existing ability (e.g. verbal, numerical or logical reasoning) in a sophisticated format, typically psychometric and usually delivered online, at least initially (some Users elect to supervise re-tests of Subjects).

– Verbal reasoning is associated with reading and understanding verbal information, using existing knowledge of language and grammar (a 'crystallised' intelligence), presented orally or in writing.

– Numerical reasoning involves applying mathematical functions in a variety of ways, to meet specific needs. As such is relies partly on learned skills (e.g. addition, multiplication, subtraction) but also on fluid thinking to apply that existing knowledge appropriately to meet the need.

– Logical (inductive or deductive) reasoning is less easily taught and typically requires fluid reasoning on information presented neither verbally nor mathematically.

Although these three ability tests are the most widely used, test publishers have found other constructs which they have identified as 'abilities' and measure with psychometric validity such as 'commercial reasoning', 'proof reading', 'calculation' and 'data capture'.

These are all tests of "maximum performance", i.e. they are designed to establish how well a person can perform at their best which is why they are usually timed and have right and wrong answers.

- **Aptitude** tests:

    Assess Subject's potential to become capable of performing a function or acquiring skills; consider the extent to which the Subject is suited to a particular role/specialism/career path (e.g. working with people or numbers). Aptitude testing evaluates how Subjects accomplish tasks and react to situations they might face. The tests can include questions about interests, talents and hobbies. Schools, employment agencies and some organisations use aptitude tests to guide the test taker's professional path.

- Personality (or Preference) inventories:

    Best not referred to as a 'test', a personality inventory is a questionnaire or other standardised instrument designed to reveal aspects of an individual's character or psychological makeup. Personality tests are used in a range of contexts, including individual and relationship counselling, career planning, and employee selection and development. The most common type, the self-report inventory, involves the administration of many questions, or "items", to test-takers who respond by rating the degree to which each item reflects their preference/behaviour, and can be scored objectively. The term 'item' is used because many test questions are not actually questions; they are typically statements on questionnaires that allow respondents to indicate level of agreement.

    - Test publishers have created a wide range of application for personality inventories including, for example: leadership profilers, motivational profilers, specialist (e.g. sales) profilers, culture fit questionnaires, 'inclination to engagement' measures and strengths inventories (often associated with coaching and development guides).

    - These are 'tests' of "typical performance", i.e. they are designed to predict how a person is likely to behave across a range of situations, they are usually untimed and do not have right and wrong answers.

    - Users should be cautious in using these Assessments in recruitment as they are not measures of ability and individuals' preferences do not necessarily dictate their capability. (E.g. A Subject may say "I like to work with numbers" but this does not mean they are necessary competent in doing so, or "I prefer not to analyse information" does not mean the Subject is incapable of doing so when the need arises.)

- Situational Judgement Tests:

SJTs are a type of psychological test in which Subjects are presented with realistic, hypothetical scenarios and ask the individual to identify an appropriate response. These are generally in a multiple-choice format but represent a distinct psychometric approach from the common knowledge-based multiple-choice item as the desirability of responses can be determined and scored.

Unlike most psychological tests SJTs are seldom acquired off-the-shelf in the UK, but are more often designed as a bespoke tool, tailor-made to suit specific role/job family requirements. Some-off-the-shelf options do exist however, e.g. for "leadership" or "customer contact."

SJTs are often useful in instances where Subjects may have no/minimal previous experience of the roles' requirements, so immersing them in hypothetical situations allows the Users to gather evidence that would not otherwise be available.

– Realistic Job Previews

RJPs are essentially the same sort of tool as an SJT. They are named this way because they intentionally provide Subjects with an insight into a role or activity's requirements. They can be used before formal Assessments to encourage Subjects to 'self-select' whether they are a good fit for particular organisations, roles, or job families. They can be used to 'sell' the best aspects of a job or caution Subjects regarding the 'worst' or most challenging aspects of a role.

– Capability-based questions:

Discussed in detail in the previous section. These can be used on forms, during interviews, or combined with other Assessment approaches.

– In-tray exercises:

Usually ask Subjects to assume a particular role as an employee of a fictitious organisation and to work through a pile of correspondence in an 'in-tray' (including, for example, e-mail messages, faxes, memos, letters, telephone messages, reports, articles and so on). This typically simulates the administrative features of a particular role. (This can be done on a PC with automated/interactive items or on paper.) The in-tray exercise items are usually specifically designed to measure job skills such as the ability to analyse information, organise and prioritise work and allocate responsibility for tasks; in-tray exercises may also have a written component.

- **Role-play** exercises:

Subjects are immersed in a scenario where they must meet with someone to achieve a particular objective. For example, if it is a management position the scenario may be a meeting with a demotivated staff member where the task will be to find out what problems they have and steer them back towards good performance. If the job includes sales or customer service, the meeting may be role-playing a customer; this might take place face-to-face or 'on the phone' dependent on the nature of the work to be done.

Role plays are usually used to measure capabilities such as empathy, assertiveness, prioritising and structure, negotiation and/or persuasion.

- **Case study** exercises:

Subjects are given a selection of information, often more than they can necessarily evaluate in-depth in the time allowed, including for example both relevant and irrelevant facts and figures, opinions and reports, articles, correspondence and so on. Subjects must evaluate the data provided and draw conclusions, usually against a few assigned questions or themes. This form of Assessment is useful in collecting evidence of Subjects' abilities to understand, evaluate and summarise information both superficially and in-depth, analyse problems, prioritise tasks and put forward effective arguments to support their point of view.

- **Fact-find** exercises:

These take a similar format to a role play but usually require the Subject to gather specific information to achieve a particular objective. Subjects collect information by asking questions and use it to come to a decision and justify it. Observing this process can be useful in Assessing Subjects' ability to question effectively, listen actively, looking for patterns or inconsistencies and identify 'openings' provided by the role player to gain additional insight. They may also include commercial, strategic, and/or problem-solving elements and a second part in which Subjects report back on their findings. These are similar to, and sometimes also referred to as, "Analysis Exercises" in which Subjects review information about a company and generate either a presentation or written report.

- **Presentation** exercises:

    Often associated with a case study, fact-find or analysis exercise, Subjects are required to 'present' their view/findings on a topic. This may be to a single Assessor or audience/group of people/Assessors.

- **Written** exercises:

    Often associated with a case study, fact-find or analysis exercise, Subjects are required to provide their view/findings on a topic in writing.

- Group discussion/task exercises:

    These Assessments are usually concerned with collaboration, consultation, planning and organising, and problem solving. In most cases, the group are required only to analyse, discuss and solve a problem/scenario. But practical tasks can also be used, in which the group are also required to act on their solution to produce a specific outcome (e.g. create an advertisement).

    Group tasks take various forms, for example:

    - Assigned roles: Subjects are each given a 'position', 'character' or 'role' to play during a discussion. Subjects are usually asked to negotiate with others in the group and argue a case for their own role/position.

    - Unassigned roles: Subjects are placed in a group to discuss a topic, problem or situation. The group collectively agree on how to proceed in identifying the best course of action to meet shared goals.

- 360-degree feedback surveys:

    These are not suitable for recruitment but can offer value to development and coaching programmes. The 360-degree (360°) process begins with collecting feedback from peers, clients, colleagues and managers who Assess the Subject against a relevant construct (e.g. behaviours, competencies or values). This is a two-part process (at least) as the feedback, once collected, must form the basis of coaching and/or development planning. Often this cycle is repeated periodically (e.g. annually) to measure progress and refocus development plans. The time required for multiple parties to complete the feedback surveys should be accounted for and individuals should be given clarity on the purpose and value of the measure as well as support in realising the benefits.

Collection of fewer perspectives are often referred to a **180° or 270° feedback** exercises.

– Other Assessment tools can be used to Assess teams, to build their effectiveness and increase collaboration and productivity between members. Organisational tools such as culture or engagement surveys can also be valuable. These will not be addressed in detail here but could be considered to complement other Assessment activities, when Subjects are existing employees, as they can support the organisation in measuring impact and the return on investment for individual Assessment activities.

What has not been discussed here (i.e. not within the remit of this document) are practical Subject eligibility/suitability verification interventions, such as reference checking, credit/background checks, qualification verification, criminal record searches, etc. often associated with recruitment.

Applications for Assessment

Assessment is applied in two contexts: (1) most commonly to support recruitment activities by establishing the relative suitability of Subjects for job roles, and also (2) in change and/or development processes, where existing employees are Assessed for benchmarking, learning needs analysis, development, redeployment, transition or workforce reduction.

There are many overlaps in the tools and processes that apply to these two different contexts (applications). Some are more useful in one or another context. In this section we'll discuss **factors to consider when making decisions about which Assessment(s) to use**.

Factors to Consider

Is the Assessment **resource intensive or resource light**?

– The resources required for Assessment administration should be considered to the fullest extent, including: time required of the

User, time required of the Subject, technology requirements, venue demands, training requirements and direct costs (e.g. for development and/or usage/licenses).

– Ability tests can carry direct costs and technology requirement but may be 'resource light' (relatively quick and cost effective) for the User to administer. Group exercises are resource intensive as they require development and/or license costs, administration venues, User (Assessor and administrator) time for training, preparation, delivery and follow up, travel time and costs for 'in person' attendance, etc. For this reason, ability tests are usually used for large pools of Subjects whilst group exercises are used only when the Subject pool has been reduced. In this context also consider 'distribution' of your Subject pool, i.e. how realistic is it to have all Subjects interacting face-to-face with Assessors and/or how likely are Subjects to have access to relevant technology?

– When considering the level of resources available/required, consider the anticipated value of achieving the best Assessment outcomes. Your investments in Assessment should always provide a reasonable return by, for example, increasing productivity/efficiency, reducing risk of poor hiring decisions, improving team performance, etc. For example, in a hiring context there is evidence to suggest that a poor hiring decision may 'cost' an organisation the equivalent of the poor hire's annual salary. It stands to reason therefore that the higher the salary scale associated with the recruitment activity (i.e. the more senior the appointment), the greater the risk if a poor decision is made; investing more in Assessing for senior roles may therefore stand to reason.

Can a **generic** Assessment be used, or is there a case for **branding/customisation**?

– When Assessing for recruitment and dealing with large volumes of candidates or within highly competitive talent markets, entrenching your brand in the tools used can support you in engaging candidates and helping them recognise your process as distinctive. The extent to which you 'brand' your tools/processes can vary in complexity and cost but would usually incur at least some expense.

– On the topic of branding, consider seriously the intended and unintended messages Assessment Subjects will get through the process. For example, 'cheap' looking tools would be inappropriate in a leadership development setting, 'glossy' tools may be inappropriate in a not-for-profit or public sector setting, etc. Equally, it would be incongruent for an organisation in the technology sector to use a mostly manual (off-line) process.

- Beyond specific tools, your process should also reflect your brand and values accurately, for example, if your brand messaging is around corporate responsibility and/or ethical behaviour, you cannot afford to have an Assessment process that is not clear and transparent, fails to support candidate progression, excludes feedback provision or makes it difficult for Subjects to arrange necessary consideration (such as reasonable adjustments) in the process.

Who will be taking the Assessment? Are the audience more **junior** or **senior**?

- Consider the Subject's level of experience, expertise and expectation of challenge. Some tools (e.g. SJTs) are particularly well suited to use with less experienced Subjects whilst others (e.g. case studies) are particularly useful in stretching Assessments of more experienced Subjects.

- Higher levels of expenditure on Assessment may be more easily justified if the business is already investing highly in the Subjects, e.g. senior leadership recruitment or development (as opposed to entry level clerical staff) or relationship management specialists (as opposed to back office staff).

Will the Assessment be required to **standalone**, or be used in **combination** with other Assessments?

- If a tool is to be used in isolation, it should be particularly robust and highly relevant to the Assessment purpose. More often a combination of tools is used, progressively or simultaneously, which each contribute different value to the Assessment process (e.g. ability tests and interviews, or Assessment centres which feature a collection of observed activities).

- Within recruitment contexts, a sequential Assessment process is usually used to reduce Subject numbers with increasingly complex/resource demanding tools.

- In a development context it is important to consider what information already exists regarding the Subject(s) to ensure that the Assessment tools used complement it rather than outweighing or contradicting it. Information collected over a longer period will often have more face validity for Subjects (e.g. an annual performance appraisal vs. a half day Assessment centre).

Is the intention of the Assessment to **identify weakness**, or **recognise strengths**? This consideration applies at two levels:

– First, are you looking for reasons to 'progress' Subjects or reasons to 'reject' them? The use of Assessment tools for deselection is different from using them to 'select the best'. The question to ask would be: Do you want to remove the people at the bottom of the pile (in terms of fit/suitability) or identify the people at the top of the pile? The outcome may seem the same, but the motivation is important to understand. Do you have 1,000 candidates and you need to hire 950 – or do you have a pool of 100 and you need to hire one? Deselection tools (e.g. to remove 50% of candidates from the pool quickly), include, for example, skills and ability tests which can identify weakness in Subjects. Selection tools (e.g. to identify the best 10% of candidates), often include personality inventories, interviews and Assessment centres.

– Second, are you focusing on strength or weakness? 'Positive psychology' and 'strengths-based' Assessment and development interventions are increasingly popular in Business Psychology. These approaches can be particularly helpful in development settings but are also relevant to recruitment Assessments. Focusing on strengths in your process (e.g. seeking to evaluate how past experience might be of value in a new/future setting) is similar to using a 'selection' mind-set; whilst focusing on weaknesses (e.g. to reduce risks of poor hiring decisions by removing unsuitable candidates) in some respects denotes a 'deselection' mind-set.

Will Subjects consider the Assessment **routine**, or **exceptional**?

– The context in which the Assessment will be carried out should be considered. Assessment in recruitment is fairly routine in many lands so many candidates expect it. Nevertheless, some candidates (e.g. very senior executives) may not expect to be Subjected to batteries of tests and several stages of deselection. Graduates on the other hand would expect in most cases nothing less than a few stages of Assessment prior to hiring.

– In an 'internal' context, for example when the Assessment is being undertaken for the sake of capability-building, population diagnostics, to reorganise or reduce teams/staff, Subjects may be more sensitive, and greater care may be required. For example, the face validity of tools and relevance to the roles/context must be explicit and the use of a combination of tools and sources of information should be considered (e.g. as mentioned previously, annual performance appraisal data should be evaluated alongside other data collected from Assessment activities).

- Be aware that consultation with the staff groups concerned and/or Unions may be appropriate/required and that justification of each of the tools selected will be essential to the success of the initiative and Subjects' acceptance of outcomes. Staff groups/Unions often respond well to an organisation's commitment to engage objective third-party Assessors in these processes.

Is the Assessment environment likely to be **low risk** or **high risk**?

- Bear in mind that no Assessment will be fool-proof or complete in identifying every detail or risk associated with the performance being Assessed.
- If you are Assessing in a 'high risk' context, e.g. for very senior roles, in a highly competitive market, for business-critical talent or to reduce your work-force, consider all of the factors above and include combinations of Assessment.
- In high risk contexts it can be useful to organisations to engage objective third-party Assessors as advisors and/or deliverers to ensure standards are high and consistent.

Applications for Assessment

Users of Assessment tools and processes have a wide range of reasons for doing so. The sustainability of all commercial operations is dependent to at least some extent on the ability of its staff to work in support of its strategic objectives. Organisations need insight into the extent to which their people (current or prospective) are able and willing to do work assigned to them, in an optimal and sustainable manner.

Assessment tools and processes can provide relevant, valid, tangible information which can inform sound commercial decisions regarding investments in skills training, capability building, succession planning, team building, hiring and so on. They can also supply evidence of the effectiveness of any/all of these decisions /investments once delivered.

The use of Assessments to gain an insight into the quality and value of an organisation's human capital can mitigate, to some extent, the risks inherent in relying on people to sustain a commercial enterprise. At best, it can offer opportunities for defining and creating a distinctive, highly productive, effective, efficient, innovative, strategically aligned and customer-satisfying workforce.

The questions below serve as useful prompts for creating or recognising when Assessment may be the best practice response to a situation, improving outcomes and/or reducing risk.

- What measures are in place to ensure critical hiring decisions are supported with effective, objective and consistent processes?

    Introducing Assessment tools to recruitment is extremely common practice and can be done very cost effectively. The reduction of risks associated with 'bad' hiring is of immediate advantage to organisations.

- How is the success and value of training, learning and development spend being measured?

    Assessments before, during and/or after these interventions can support needs analysis and help quantify benefits/successes.

- How standardised and objective are current performance management practices? What proactive steps has the organisation taken to measure, benchmark and report on people's contributions, effectiveness and value to the organisation? What has this revealed? How has action been taken to address opportunities that have arisen?

    Assessments before, during and/or after these interventions can support accurate appraisals and reward decision making.

- How are succession-planning decisions being made?

    Assessments can be used to challenge or confirm that individuals within your leadership/specialist pipeline are both qualified for greater responsibility and have the potential to be successful in increasingly senior/demanding roles.

- Creating/recognising strategic opportunities

    How do you know if your teams/individuals are operating at their peak of performance? Assessments can be used to compare and contrast current performance with potential.

- Which business areas are underperforming?

    Individual, team, leadership or organisational Assessments can be used to identify the source/cause of underperformance and provide a starting point to addressing issues.

- Where is the business most at risk if people are underperforming / lost?

    Assessments can be used to identify accurately exactly which skills and capabilities are essential to success in those areas to create a sustainable pipeline for the talent pool.

    Assessment and development of leadership capability to support, engage and motivate individuals in these roles can reduce the likelihood of losing talented individuals.

    Culture and/or engagement surveys can provide information which organisations can use to inform initiatives which create stability and longevity in these environments as well.

- Which functions are likely to be increasingly or decreasingly important in the future?

    Assessments can provide clarity for the organisation as to whether the current workforce have the necessary skills and capabilities to increase their contribution in line with business requirements and/or ascertain if individuals who may no longer be required in their current roles could be effectively redeployed.

- What will be the organisation's biggest 'people' challenge in the next one to three years?

    Identification of skills/capability gaps between the current ('as is') business model and strategic vision for the future state is critical if the future state is to be realised. Accurate identification of staff capability and skill needs – and leadership requirements – will allow for proactive capability and skill building in support of business objectives.

    For example, most organisations anticipate increasingly fast-paced change and ambiguity in the future. Are their people equipped for that, resilient and able to cope with this? Assessments could give confidence or early warnings.

Considerations in Clarifying Opportunities

Before undertaking Assessment activities, the purpose and motivation should be clearly understood and communicated. Questions to answer before undertaking these activities might include:

- What is the purpose of this Assessment and what is the required output? (e.g. time saving, cost saving, risk reduction, reduced attrition, increased sales revenue, speed of new joiners achieving full effectiveness)

- Who owns this activity/process, i.e. is accountable for its success, the data collected and the results to be delivered?
- Is there senior (leadership) support for this activity?
- When/how will the approach/process be piloted, trialled, implemented, delivered and reviewed?
- Is there sufficient resource and infrastructure in place to deliver this properly?
- How will the information collected be used?
- What will success look like? (in terms of process and performance outcomes)
- How will success be measured?
- What existing information could complement, confirm or contradict Assessment findings?
- Is the solution proposed sustainable (if necessary)?
- Is the scale appropriate?
- Is this activity aligned to the wider organisation's priorities and strategy?
- What guidance is in place to ensure Subjects benefit from this experience?
- What are the Subjects' expectations?
- What value will this offer the individuals, teams, leadership and/or organisation concerned?
- What impact is this likely to have on the business?
- How will this contribute to the organisation's success?
- What risks are associated with this intervention?

Other Considerations

Communicating about Assessment

In all applications of Assessment, it is best to be clear and transparent about your motivations for using Assessment tools and the Assessments you derive from them. For recruitment, this may be information provided on your website or candidate communications. For development this will usually be a feature of line manager activity, supported by HR and/or other context specific messaging. Always plan this communication carefully and ensure it is delivered effectively.

Maximising the Benefits of Assessment

Best practice also suggests that feedback should always be provided to Subjects, in writing or orally. This is fundamental and essential in a development context and highly desirable in a recruitment process as a 'duty of care' to candidates. By disclosing a Subject's Assessment results you can address any concerns or scepticism they may have regarding the Assessment content or process. If the test taker has a clear understanding of how the data from the test session is being used within the process, equal opportunities and fairness are promoted. Additionally, a feedback discussion can also be an opportunity for the User to verify the results presented in the Assessment. The interpreter may relate the results to the test takers' experiences in the workplace. It also provides the interpreter with the opportunity to check if there were any special circumstances surrounding the time that the Subject took the tests that may have affected the way they performed.